GREAT
FREETHINKERS

GREAT FREETHINKERS

Selected Quotations By Famous Skeptics & Nonconformists

Edited by
James C. Sanford

METACOMET BOOKS ~ PROVIDENCE
2004

Published by Metacomet Books
P.O. Box 2479
Providence, Rhode Island 02906
(401) 421-5750
www.metacometbooks.com

ISBN: 0-9747042-3-7 (Hardcover)
ISBN: 0-9747042-2-9 (Paperback)

LCCN: 2003116673

Second Printing: 2006

Book design: Janice Phelps
Some images © 2003 www.clipart.com
Cover illustration based on a figure of Voltaire at the
Musée de l'Histoire de Paris

PRINTED IN THE UNITED STATES ON ACID-FREE PAPER

This book is dedicated to Salman Rushdie and Taslima Nasrin, two contemporary freethinkers who by challenging religious and cultural taboos have contributed to the freedom of all people.

Contents

Contents

Preface

The freethinkers whose quotations appear in this book constitute a small but conspicuous minority in the annals of history. They are a minority by choice, known for their plainspoken honesty and willingness to grapple with difficult truths. Indeed, their independence sometimes brought them in conflict with the dearly held creeds and conventions of their times, often at great peril to themselves. For centuries the opinions of freethinkers raised the hackles of mainstreamers and provoked establishment forces. Even today, when most forms of expression are better tolerated, their words generate controversy.

The term "freethinker" broadly designates a person who thinks independently and refuses to take on faith the claims of authority. The term was first employed in 17th and 18th century England to describe those inquirers who tested the hallowed ground of religion and dared to reach their own conclusions about it. In the lexicons of the orthodox, the word became a term of reproach and for years was used as a synonym for "atheist."

Although many freethinkers can be described as atheists, the two words are not identical. Bertrand Russell properly characterizes "freethought" as denoting not so much one's beliefs as the way in which one holds them. If beliefs are held in deference to some external authority, scriptural or otherwise, or simply as a means of bringing peace of mind, they cannot be said to be freely held. On the other hand, if beliefs are based solely on weighing the evidence wherever it may lead, then they can be considered freely held regardless of the oddity of one's conclusions.

Religion was just one form of authority questioned by freethinkers. Freethinking dissidents challenged the state in the name of freedom and social justice. Reformers and revolutionaries contested the traditional economic order and the rule of class privilege. Scientists resisted the Church-supported world view. Artists broke taboos and explored new forms of expression. A roster of names in this collection – among them Rousseau, Wollstonecraft, Jefferson, Thoreau, Darwin, Nietzsche, Freud, and Einstein – reveals some of the prime movers of modern civilization.

Almost 200 men and women are represented in this book. They hold a variety of philosophical viewpoints, although all bring to the world some measure of skepticism. They include atheists, agnostics, rationalists, humanists, and an assortment of unconventional theists. Politically they cover the ground from classical liberalism to socialism and anarchism. They find themselves labelled as nonconformists, heretics, dissidents, bohemians, and radicals. If they frequently disagree among themselves, it is because such is the nature of freethinking. There is no "creed" of freethought.

I have used several criteria for the inclusion of quotations, the most important being the incisiveness and depth of the views expressed and the eloquence of expression. Humor and irony are a factor in many of the choices. In general I have favored novelty and freshness over familiarity. The reader may notice the omission of a few quotations which have become so familiar, even trite, that they have lost most of their original impact. Marx's "Religion is the opium of the people," for example, has been excluded for this reason. Conversely, numerous quotations not present in previous anthologies have been included in the hope that they will find greater acceptance.

The reader will notice that the language of some of the quotations shows gender bias, fairly common in classical writers. In other cases, the language is stilted and arcane. Generally I have edited with a light hand, occasionally adjusting the punctuation when clarity is at stake and using ellipses in the interests of conciseness, but otherwise leaving the text as originally formulated for readers to use as they see fit.

It should be obvious that the selected quotations are only a bare sampling of what is available. This collection does not pretend to be authoritative, and some readers may justly claim to know of better quotations and of authors unduly excluded. I hope they will contact me so that I can make use of their suggestions for future editions.

For whom was this book created? Many quotation books are aimed primarily at casual users and those who employ them primarily as tools for use in articles, speeches, and reference research. Certainly this collection addresses itself to those uses. But above all it was created for readers: readers with an irreverent bent and an appreciation for the pithy expression of ideas. I have made an effort to pinpoint the sources of quotations as precisely as possible to allow the reader to go back to the original works. The purpose of this book would surely be achieved if it helped to revive interest in some of these great past and present thinkers.

I wish to acknowledge the help of many in this project. I owe a large debt, first of all, to all the compilers of books of quotations who have preceded me. Their efforts provided the initial inspiration and foundation for this collection. In getting access to the primary sources necessary for a more intensive sifting of the literature, I benefitted greatly from the friendly assistance of the librarians at Brown's Rockefeller Library and those at the Fox Point Branch of the Providence Library. Many colleagues and friends have been generous with their advice, especially John Harkey, John Loge, and Bernard Unti. My thanks to Laird Wilcox for kindly helping me navigate some of the publishing issues involved, and to Jim Haught and Annie Laurie Gaylor for taking the time to read the manuscript.

Also to Janice Phelps, who has been invaluable in moving this book through every stage of the production process. Her art work for the book speaks for itself. I thank Jean for being a patient sounding board for many of my crazy ideas, and Mel for her enthusiasm and support. I am especially grateful to Andrew, who carefully critiqued the manuscript, suggested improvements, and caused me to rethink many of my assumptions.

Knowledge
&
Ethics

Mind. Thought

The effort at understanding is the first and single basis of virtue, and we should not endeavor to understand things for the sake of any ulterior object.
—BENEDICT DE SPINOZA, *Ethics*, IV, 26, 1677

There is a small number of men and women who think for all the others, and for whom all the rest talk and act.
—JEAN-JACQUES ROUSSEAU, *Julie ou la nouvelle Héloise*, II, 14, 1761

Enlightenment is man's emergence from his self-incurred tutelage. Tutelage is man's inability to make use of his understanding without direction from another. And this tutelage is self-incurred when it is caused by the lack, not of understanding, but of the resolution and courage to use it without direction from another. *Sapere aude!* Have the courage to use your own understanding! – that is the motto of the Enlightenment.
—IMMANUEL KANT, "What Is Enlightenment?" *Berlinischer Monatsschrift*, 1784

I made the journey to knowledge like dogs who go for walks with their masters, a hundred times forward and backward over the same territory; and when I arrived I was tired.
—CHRISTOF LICHTENBERG, *Aphorisms*, in Mautner & Hatfield, eds., *The Lichtenberg Reader* (1959), 1789

I do not believe that any two men, on what are called doctrinal points, think alike who think at all. It is only those who have not thought that appear to agree.
—THOMAS PAINE, *The Rights of Man*, II, 1792

Let the human mind loose. It must be loose. It will be loose. Superstition and dogmatism cannot confine it.
—JOHN ADAMS, letter to his son, John Quincy Adams, November 13, 1816

The truest state of mind, rested in, becomes false. Thought is the manna which cannot be stored. It will be sour if kept, and tomorrow must be gathered anew.
—RALPH WALDO EMERSON, *Journals*, May 13, 1835

The mind of man is like a clock that is always running down, and requires to be as constantly wound up.
—WILLIAM HAZLITT, *Sketches and Essays*, "Cant and Hypocrisy," 1839

We come down with freethinking into the dear institutions and at once make carnage amongst them. We are innocent of any such fell purpose as the sequel seems to impute to us. We were only smoking a cigar, but it turns out to be a powder mill that we are promenading.
—RALPH WALDO EMERSON, *Journals*, September-November, 1843

Knowledge & Ethics

Why level downward to our dullest perception always, and praise that as common sense? The commonest sense is the sense of men asleep, which they express by snoring.
—HENRY DAVID THOREAU, *Walden*, "Conclusion," 1854

The fatal tendency of mankind to leave off thinking about a thing when it is no longer doubtful, is the cause of half their errors. A contemporary author has well spoken of "the deep slumber of a decided opinion."
—JOHN STUART MILL, *On Liberty*, 2, 1859

Thought, the gaseous ashes of burned-out thinking, the excretion of mental respiration.
—OLIVER WENDELL HOLMES, *The Professor at the Breakfast-Table*, 1, 1860

Nothing more clearly separates a vulgar from a superior mind than the confusion in the first between the little that it truly knows, on the one hand, and what it half knows and what it thinks it knows on the other.
—OLIVER WENDELL HOLMES, *Border Lines of Knowledge in some Provinces of Medical Science*, 1862

Is it then a matter of arriving at that view of God, world, and reconciliation which makes us feel most comfortable? Rather, isn't the true inquirer wholly indifferent to the result of his inquiries?
—FRIEDRICH NIETZSCHE, letter to Elisabeth Nietzsche (Kaufmann transl.), June 11, 1865

Banish me from Eden when you will, but first let me eat of the fruit of the tree of knowledge.
—ROBERT G. INGERSOLL, *The Gods*, 1872

We call that man a freethinker who thinks otherwise than is expected of him in respect to his origins, surroundings, position, and office, or in respect to the prevailing contemporary views. He is the exception, the fettered minds are the rule.
—FRIEDRICH NIETZSCHE, *Human All Too Human*, 225, 1878

To the mass of people nothing is so costly as thought. The fact that, taking the world over, ninety-nine people out of a hundred accept the creed to which they were born, exemplifies their mental attitude towards things at large.
—HERBERT SPENCER, *The Principles of Ethics*, 435, 1892

For my part, I have no excessive confidence in reason. I know how weak and tottering it is. But I remember Diderot's clever apologue: "I have," he said, "only a small flickering light to guide me in the darkness of a thick forest. Up comes a theologian and blows it out." Let us first of all follow reason, it is the surest guide.
—ANATOLE FRANCE, *The Opinions of Anatole France*, "The Credo of a Sceptic," 1921

The brain can be developed just the same as the muscles can be developed, if one will only take the pains to train the mind to think.
—THOMAS A. EDISON, *The Diary and Sundry Observations* (1948), 1921

Thinking is learning all over again to see, to be attentive, to focus consciousness; it is turning every idea and every image . . . into a privileged moment.
—ALBERT CAMUS, *The Myth of Sisyphus*, "An Absurd Reasoning," 1942

If devotion to truth is the hallmark of morality, then there is no greater, nobler, more heroic form of devotion than the act of a man who assumes the responsibility of thinking.
—AYN RAND, *Atlas Shrugged*, 1957

What makes a freethinker is not his beliefs but the way in which he holds them. If he holds them because his elders told him they were true when he was young, or if he holds them because if he did not he would be unhappy, his thought is not free; but if he holds them because, after careful thought he finds a balance of evidence in their favor, then his thought is free, however odd his conclusions may seem.
— BERTRAND RUSSELL, *Understanding History*, "The Value of Free Thought," 1957

The beginning of thought is in disagreement – not only with others but also with ourselves.
—ERIC HOFFER, *The Passionate State of Mind*, 266, 1955

It is time at least to suggest a wider connection between rationality in general and personal integrity. . . . To the extent that I make claims to knowledge without ensuring that I am indeed in a position to know, I must prejudice my claims both to sincerity and ingenuousness.
—ANTONY FLEW, *Thinking About Thinking*, 8, 1975

There are no dangerous thoughts; thinking itself is dangerous.
—HANNAH ARENDT, *The New Yorker*, December 5, 1977

Truth

As for certain truth, no man has seen it, nor will there ever be a man who knows about the gods and about all the things I mention.
—XENOPHANES, Fragments (Freeman transl.), 6th Century B.C.

My plainness of speech makes them hate me, and what is their hatred but a proof that I am speaking the truth?
—SOCRATES, quoted in Plato's *Apology*, 4th century B.C.

There is no more natural desire than the desire for knowledge. We attempt all means that may bring us to it. When reason fails us, we employ experience . . . which is a feebler and less worthy means. But truth is so great a thing that we must not disdain any medium that will lead us to it.
—MICHEL DE MONTAIGNE, *Essays*, III, 13, 1588

Truth has to overcome a thousand obstacles to get on paper undamaged, and back from the paper to the mind.
—GEORG CHRISTOF LICHTENBERG, *Aphorisms*, in Mautner & Hatfield, eds., *The Lichtenberg Reader* (1959), 1773–75

Knowledge & Ethics

It is error alone which needs the support of government. Truth can stand by itself.
—THOMAS JEFFERSON, *Notes on the State of Virginia*, 17, 1787

The blackest billingsgate, the most ungentlemanly insolence, the most yahooish brutality is patiently endured, countenanced, propagated, and applauded. But touch a solemn truth in collision with a dogma of a sect, though capable of the clearest proof, and you will soon find you have disturbed a nest, and the hornets will swarm about your legs and hands, and fly into your face and eyes.
—JOHN ADAMS, letter to John Taylor, 1814

Truth is at variance with our natures, but not so error; and for a very simple reason. Truth requires us to recognize ourselves as limited; but error flatters us with the belief that in one way or another we are subject to no bounds at all.
—JOHANN WOLFGANG VON GOETHE, *Maxims and Reflections*, 310, 1826

He in whom the love of truth predominates will keep himself aloof from all moorings, and afloat. . . . He submits to the inconveniences of suspense and imperfect opinion, but he is a candidate for truth.
—RALPH WALDO EMERSON, *Essays*, First Series, "Intellect," 1841

To free a man from error is to give, not take away. Knowledge that a thing is false is a truth.
—ARTHUR SCHOPENHAUER, *Parerga and Paralipomena*, Vol. II, 15, 1851

Truth that has been merely learned is like an artificial limb, a false tooth, a waxen nose; at best like a nose made out of another's flesh; it adheres to us only because it is put on. But truth acquired by thinking of our own is like a natural limb; it alone really belongs to us.
—ARTHUR SCHOPENHAUER, *Parerga and Paralipomena*, Vol. II, 22, 1851

Even if the received opinion be not only true, but the whole truth; unless it is . . . vigorously and earnestly contested, it will, by most of those who receive it, be held in the manner of a prejudice, with little comprehension or feeling of its rational grounds.
—JOHN STUART MILL, *On Liberty*, 2, 1859

In proportion as we love truth more and victory less, we shall become anxious to know what it is which leads our opponents to think as they do.
—HERBERT SPENCER, *First Principles*, 3, 1862

Here the ways of men divide. If you want to achieve peace of mind and happiness, then have faith; if you want to be a disciple of truth, then search.
—FRIEDRICH NIETZSCHE, letter to Elisabeth Nietzsche (Middleton transl.), June 11, 1865

I hate . . . the artists and critics who foolishly wish to fashion the truth of the present out of the truth of the past. They do not understand that we progress and that the scenery changes.
—ÉMILE ZOLA, *Mes haines*, "Preface," 1866

The pathos of *possessing* truth is now of very little consequence in comparison with the certainly milder and less noisy pathos of searching for truth, which is never weary of learning and examining afresh.
—FRIEDRICH NIETZSCHE, *Human All Too Human*, 633, 1878

Convictions are more dangerous enemies of truth than lies.
—FRIEDRICH NIETZSCHE, *Human All Too Human*, 483, 1878

A man should never put on his best trousers when he goes out to battle for freedom and truth.
—HENRIK IBSEN, *An Enemy of the People*, V, 1882

He who sets out to search for Truth must leave these valleys of Superstition forever, taking with him not one shred that has belonged to them. Alone he must wander down into the Land of Absolute Negation and Denial. He must abide there. He must resist temptation. When the light breaks he must arise and follow it into the country of dry sunshine. The mountains of stern Reality will rise before him. He must climb them. *Beyond* them lies Truth.
—OLIVE SCHREINER, *The Story of an African Farm*, II, 2, 1883

It is wrong for a man to say that he is certain of the objective truth of any proposition unless he can produce evidence which logically justifies that certainty. This is what agnosticism asserts.
—THOMAS H. HUXLEY, *Collected Essays*, Vol. V, "Agnosticism and Christianity," 1889

Nathaniel, throw away my book; do not let it satisfy you. Do not believe that *your* truth can be discovered by anyone else.
—ANDRÉ GIDE, *Fruits of the Earth*, "Envoi," 1897

Familiarity breeds contempt. How accurate that is. The reason we hold truth in such respect is because we have so little opportunity to get familiar with it.
—MARK TWAIN, *Mark Twain's Notebook* (1935), Summer, 1898

We divert our attention from disease and death as much as we can; and the slaughter-houses and indecencies without end on which our life is founded are huddled out of sight and never mentioned, so that the world we recognize officially in literature and in society is a poetic fiction far handsomer and cleaner and better than the world that really is.
—WILLIAM JAMES, *The Varieties of Religious Experience*, 4 & 5, 1902

To have to distinguish fact from fancy is so great a violence to the inner man that not only poets, but theologians and philosophers, still protest against such a distinction.
—GEORGE SANTAYANA, *Reason in Art*, 6, 1905

If you demand my authorities for this and that, I must reply that only those who have never hunted up the authorities as I have believe that there is any authority who is not contradicted flatly by some other authority.
—GEORGE BERNARD SHAW, *Androcles and the Lion*, "Preface," 1912

Nature does not seem to care very much whether our ideas are true or not, as long as we get on through life safely enough. And it is surprising on what an enormous amount of error we can get along comfortably.
—RANDOLPH BOURNE, *Youth and Life*, "The Life of Irony," 1913

The final test of truth is ridicule. Very few religious dogmas have ever faced it and survived.
—H. L. MENCKEN, *Damn! A Book of Calumny*, 25, 1918

I love truth. I believe humanity has need of it. But assuredly humanity has much greater need still of the untruth which flatters it, consoles it, gives it infinite hopes.
—ANATOLE FRANCE, *La Vie en Fleur*, 1922

Nine times out of ten, in the arts as in life, there is actually no truth to be discovered; there is only error to be exposed.
—H. L. MENCKEN, *Prejudices*, Third Series, 1922

The truth is not itself luminous, as wit is; the truth travels silently in the night and requires to be caught by the searchlight of wit to become visible.
—GEORGE SANTAYANA, *Soliloquies in England and Later Soliloquies*, 13, 1922

I would lay siege to the truth only as animal exploration and fancy may do so, first from one quarter and then from another, expecting the reality to be not simpler than my experience of it, but far more extensive and complex.
—GEORGE SANTAYANA, *Scepticism and Animal Faith*, "Preface," 1923

Great Freethinkers

Make any statement that is so true that it has been staring us in the face all our lives, and the whole world will rise up and passionately contradict you. If you don't withdraw and apologize, it will be the worse for you. But just tell a thundering silly lie that everyone knows is a lie, and a murmur of pleased assent will hum up from every quarter of the globe.
—GEORGE BERNARD SHAW, Aubrey in *Too True to be Good*, 1934

There are very few human beings who receive the truth, complete and staggering, by instant illumination. Most of them acquire it fragment by fragment, on a small scale, by successive developments, cellularly, like a laborious mosaic.
—ANAÏS NIN, *The Diary of Anaïs Nin*, Vol. III (1969), fall, 1943

There are trivial truths and the great truths. The opposite of a trivial truth is plainly false. The opposite of a great truth is also true.
—NIELS BOHR, *New York Times Book Review*, October 20, 1957

The aspiration for truth . . . involves self-assertion and rebellion. We refuse to be imposed upon; we refuse to be like objects; we aspire toward a higher state of being.
—WALTER KAUFMANN, *Critique of Religion and Philosophy*, III, 23, 1958

Truth and meaning are not the same. The basic fallacy . . . is to interpret meaning on the model of truth.
—HANNAH ARENDT, *The Life of the Mind*, Vol. I, "Introduction," 1978

Character. Virtue

To be able to practice five virtues everywhere in the world constitutes humanity: . . . courtesy, magnanimity, good faith, diligence, and kindness.
—CONFUCIUS, *Analects* (De Bary transl.), XVII, 6, 6th-5th century B.C.

We can experience fear, confidence, desire, anger, pity, and generally any kind of pleasure and pain either too much or too little, and in either case not properly. But to experience all this at the right time, toward the right objects, toward the right people, for the right reason, and in the right manner – that is the median and the best course.
—ARISTOTLE, *Nicomachean Ethics*, 2, 4th century B.C.

Men who are governed by reason, that is, who seek their own interest after the guidance of reason, desire nothing for themselves which they desire not for other men, and consequently are just, faithful, and honorable.
—BENEDICT DE SPINOZA, *Ethics*, IV, 18, "Note," 1677

He who lives under the guidance of reason endeavors as far as possible to render back love, or kindness, for other men's hatred, anger, contempt towards him.
—BENEDICT DE SPINOZA, *Ethics*, IV, 46, 1677

When one wishes to improve the incorrigible defects in men and circumstances, one wastes one's time and makes things worse. One should accept these faults as given and then try to counterbalance them.
—JOHANN WOLFGANG VON GOETHE, diary entry, December 14, 1778

Inequality of rank must ever impede the growth of virtue, by vitiating the mind that submits or domineers.
—MARY WOLLSTONECRAFT, *Vindication of the Rights of Men*, 1790

Independence I have long considered as the grand blessing of life, the basis of every virtue.
—MARY WOLLSTONECRAFT, *A Vindication of the Rights of Woman*, preface addressed to Talleyrand, 1792

A thing moderately good is not so good as it ought to be. Moderation in temper is always a virtue; but moderation in principle is always a vice.
—THOMAS PAINE, *Rights of Man*, II, 1792

As a botanist knows a plant in its entirety from a single leaf; as Cuvier from a single bone constructed the whole animal, so an accurate knowledge of a man's whole character may be ascertained from a single characteristic act . . . even though the act in question is of very trifling consequence.
—ARTHUR SCHOPENHAUER, *Parerga and Paralipomena*, Vol. II, 8, "On Ethics," 1851

I do not value chiefly a man's uprightness and benevolence, which are, as it were, his stem and leaves. . . . I want the flower and fruit of a man; that some fragrance be wafted over from him to me, and some ripeness flavor our intercourse. His goodness must not be a partial and transitory act, but a constant superfluity, which costs him nothing and of which he is unconscious.
—HENRY DAVID THOREAU, *Walden*, "Economy," 1854

Every man takes care that his neighbor does not cheat him. But a day comes when he begins to care that he do not cheat his neighbor. Then all goes well.
—RALPH WALDO EMERSON, *The Conduct of Life*, "Worship," 1860

Good actions are sublimated evil ones; evil actions are coarsened, debased good ones.
—FRIEDRICH NIETZSCHE, *Human All Too Human*, 107, 1878

I love him whose soul is lavish, who wants no thanks and returns none: for he is one who always bestows and does not seek to preserve himself.
—FRIEDRICH NIETZSCHE, *Thus Spoke Zarathustra*, "Prologue," 4, 1883

The practice of that which is ethically best – what we call goodness or virtue – involves a course of conduct which, in all respects, is opposed to that which leads to success in the cosmic struggle for existence. In place of ruthless self-assertion it demands self-restraint. . . . It repudiates the gladiatorial theory of existence.
—THOMAS H. HUXLEY, *Collected Essays*, Vol. IX, "Evolution and Ethics," 1893

Virtue consists, not in abstaining from vice, but in not desiring it.
—GEORGE BERNARD SHAW, *Man and Superman*, "Maxims for Revolutionists," 1903

A man's ethical behavior should be based effectively on sympathy, education, and social ties and needs; no religious basis is necessary. Man would indeed be in a poor way if he had to be restrained by fear of punishment and hope of reward after death.
—ALBERT EINSTEIN, *Ideas and Opinions* (1954), "Religion and Science," 1930

Principles which are too abstract run aground in trying to decide action. . . . The content is always concrete and thereby unforeseeable; there is always the element of invention. The one thing that counts is knowing whether the inventing that has been done, has been done in the name of freedom.
—JEAN-PAUL SARTRE, *Existentialism is a Humanism*, "The Humanism of Existentialism," 1947

Virtue is the unfolding of the specific potentialities of every organism.
—ERICH FROMM, *Man for Himself*, II, 4, 1947

One might start from the assertion that morality, goodness, is a form of realism. The idea of a really good man living in a private dream world seems unacceptable. . . . He must know certain things about his surroundings, most obviously the existence of other people and their claims.
—IRIS MURDOCH, *Existentialists and Mystics* (1997), "On 'God' and 'Good'," 1969

Self-Knowledge

Each person is a very good subject for himself, as long as he has the ability to spy on himself up close. . . . It is a thorny undertaking, and more so than it seems, to follow a course as wandering as that of our mind, to fathom the opaque depths of its internal folds.
—MICHEL DE MONTAIGNE, *Essays*, II, 6, 1580

It also happens that I do not find myself in the place where I look; and I discover myself more by accident than by searching my judgement.
—MICHEL DE MONTAIGNE, *Essays*, I, 10, 1580

Such is the nature of men, that however they may acknowledge others to be more witty, or more eloquent, or more learned; yet they will hardly believe there be many so wise as themselves.
—THOMAS HOBBES, *Leviathan*, I, 13, 1651

One would be less apt to quarrel over matters of knowledge, their cause and explanation . . . if each person knew himself above all else, and knew to which party he belonged and what way of thinking best suited his nature.
—JOHANN WOLFGANG VON GOETHE, letter to von Leonhard, Oct. 12, 1807

It is only when one feels joy or sorrow that one knows anything about himself, and only by joy or sorrow is he instructed what to seek and what to shun.
—JOHANN WOLFGANG VON GOETHE, *Conversations with Eckermann* (1836), April 10, 1829

Bad times have a scientific value. These are occasions a good learner would not miss.
—RALPH WALDO EMERSON, *Conduct of Life*, "Considerations by the Way," 1860

Let the youthful soul look back on life with the question: what have you truly loved up to now, what has drawn your soul aloft, what has mastered it and at the same time blessed it? Set up these revered objects before you and perhaps their nature and their sequence will give you a law, the fundamental law of your own true self.
—FRIEDRICH NIETZSCHE, *Untimely Meditations* (Hollingdale transl.), "Schopenhauer as Educator," 1874

Active, successful natures act, not according to the dictum "know thyself," but as if there hovered before them the commandment: *will* a self and thou shalt *become* a self.
—FRIEDRICH NIETZSCHE, *Assorted Opinions and Maxims* (Hollingdale transl.), 366, 1879

To the experimental attitude, failure means nothing beyond a shade of regret or chagrin. Whether we win or lose, something has been learned, some insight and appreciation of the workings of others or of ourselves.
—RANDOLPH BOURNE, *Youth and Life*, "The Experimental Life," 1913

Fortunately analysis is not the only way to resolve inner conflicts. Life itself still remains a very effective therapist.
—KAREN HORNEY, *Our Inner Conflicts*, 13, 1945

Our lives teach us who we are.
—SALMAN RUSHDIE, *Independent on Sunday*, February 4, 1990

Ideals

I tell you that no greater good can happen to a person than every day to discuss human excellence and the other matters about which you have heard me arguing and examining myself and others, and that an unexamined life is not worth living.
—SOCRATES, quoted in Plato's *Apology*, 4th cent. B.C.

There is nothing so beautiful and right as to play the man well and properly; nor is there any knowledge so difficult as to know how to live this life well and naturally; and of all of our infirmities, the most inhuman is to despise our being.
—MICHEL DE MONTAIGNE, *Essays*, III, 13, 1588

I am far from despising sensual pleasures. . . . But I must confess that I find it infinitely sweeter to succor the unfortunate, to disentangle a bad business, to give helpful advice, to read some pleasant book, to take a walk with a man or woman who is dear to me, to spend a few instructive hours with my children, to write a page of good prose, to carry out my duties, or to tell her whom I love something tender and true.
—DENIS DIDEROT, *Rameau's Nephew* (Stewart & Kemp transl.), 1773

In communist society, where nobody has one exclusive sphere of activity but each can become accomplished in any branch he wishes, society regulates the general production and thus makes it possible for me to do one thing today and another tomorrow, to hunt in the morning, fish in the afternoon, rear cattle in the evening, criticize after dinner, just as I have a mind, without ever becoming hunter, fisherman, shepherd, or critic.
—KARL MARX, *The German Ideology* (1932), 1, 1845-46

That aim in life is highest which requires the highest and finest discipline. How much, what infinite, leisure it requires, as of a lifetime, to appreciate a single phenomenon! You must camp down beside it as for life, having reached your land of promise, and give yourself wholly to it. It must stand for the whole world to you, symbolical of all things.
—HENRY DAVID THOREAU, *Journal*, December 28, 1852

The longer I live, the more obvious it is to me that the most sacred act of a man's life is to say and to feel, "I believe such and such to be true." All the greatest rewards and all the heaviest penalties of existence cling about that act.
—THOMAS H. HUXLEY, letter to Charles Kingsley, September 23, 1860. Quoted in *Life and Letters of Thomas Henry Huxley* (1900)

The union of the mathematician with the poet, fervor with measure, passion with correctness, this surely is the ideal.
—WILLIAM JAMES, *Collected Essays and Reviews* (1920), "Clifford's Lectures and Essays," 1879

Happiness is the only good, reason the only torch, justice the only worship, humanity the only religion, and love the only priest.
—ROBERT G. INGERSOLL, "A Tribute to Eben Ingersoll," May 31, 1879

This is *my* good; this I love. . . . I desire it not as the law of God, nor as a human law or a human need; it is not for me a guidepost to overearths and paradises. It is an earthly virtue which I love: there is little prudence in it, and least of all the understanding of all men.
—FRIEDRICH NIETZSCHE, *Thus Spoke Zarathustra*, I, 5, 1883

Knowledge & Ethics

The object of our life is the improvement of social relations. . . . To this end we need the full development of individual service in both men and women, through education, association, freedom, work, and love – human love. To this end also we need a social motherhood.
—CHARLOTTE PERKINS GILMAN, "On Ellen Key and the Woman Movement," *The Forerunner*, February, 1913

Let us first of all follow reason, it is the surest guide. It warns us itself of its feebleness and informs us of its own limitations. Moreover, so far from being incompatible with sentiment, it leads to feeling. When we have brooded deeply, the most sceptical thinkers are seized with a profound commiseration for their fellow-men, in the face of the useless and eternal flux of the Universe. . . . It is but a step from that compassion to fraternal love, and it is easily taken.
—ANATOLE FRANCE, *The Opinions of Anatole France*, "The Credo of a Sceptic," 1921

I have never looked upon ease and happiness as ends in themselves – such an ethical basis I call the ideal of a pigsty. The ideals which have lighted my way, and time after time have given me new courage to face life cheerfully, have been Kindness, Beauty, and Truth.
—ALBERT EINSTEIN, *Ideas and Opinions* (1954), "The World as I See It," 1930

The whole thing, after all, may be put very simply. I believe that it is better to tell the truth than to lie. I believe that it is better to be free than to be a slave. And I believe that it is better to know than to be ignorant.
—H. L. MENCKEN, statement in Einstein et. al., *Living Philosophies*, 1931

Self-respect combined with a measure of self-surgery, aristocracy of mind combined with democracy of heart, forthrightness with modesty or at least with good manners, dignity with a quiet laugh, honor and honesty and decency: these are the greatest qualities that man can hope to attain.
—GEORGE JEAN NATHAN, statement in Einstein et. al., *Living Philosophies*, 1931

Mental health is characterized by the ability to love and to create, by the emergence from incestuous ties to clan and soil, by a sense of identity based on one's experience of self as the subject and agent of one's powers, by the grasp of reality inside and outside of ourselves, that is, by the development of objectivity and reason.
—ERICH FROMM, *The Sane Society*, IV, 1955

I have lived in the pursuit of a vision, both personal and social. Personal: to care for what is noble, for what is beautiful, for what is gentle; to allow moments of insight to give wisdom at more mundane times. Social: to see in imagination the society that is to be created, where individuals grow freely, and where hate and greed and envy die because there is nothing to nourish them.
—BERTRAND RUSSELL, *Portraits from Memory*, "Reflections on my Eightieth Birthday," 1956

The beginning of wisdom is the awareness that there is insufficient evidence that a god or gods have created us and the recognition that we are responsible in part for our own destiny. Human beings can achieve this good life, but it is by the cultivation of the virtues of intelligence and courage, not faith and obedience, that we will most likely be able to do so.
—PAUL KURTZ, *The Transcendental Temptation*, 1986

Religion

Religion in General

The gentleman carefully develops what is within his power, and does not desire what is from Heaven. The inferior man neglects what is within his power, and seeks for what comes from Heaven.
—HSÜN TZU, *Hsün Tzu* (De Bary transl.), 17, 3rd century B.C.

If people pray for rain and it rains, how is that? I would say: Nothing in particular. Just as when people do not pray for rain, it also rains.
—HSÜN TZU, *Hsün Tzu* (De Bary transl.), 17, 3rd century B.C.

Piety does not mean appearing regularly with veiled head . . . approaching every altar, falling prostrate on the ground, and spreading out one's palms before the statues of the gods. . . . Piety is rather being able to contemplate all things with a mind at rest.
—LUCRETIUS, *On the Nature of Things*, V, ca. 50 B.C.

If the apparent meaning of Scripture conflicts with demonstrative conclusions, it must be interpreted allegorically, i.e. metaphorically.
—AVERROËS, *On the Harmony of Religion and Philosophy*, II: "Philosophy Contains Nothing Opposed to Islam," 1179

Fear of power invisible, feigned by the mind or imagined from tales publicly allowed, [is] religion.
—THOMAS HOBBES, *Leviathan*, I, 6, 1651

The people receive religion and laws in the same way they receive coins: without examining them.
—VOLTAIRE, *Le Sottissier*, mid 18th century

Many a long dispute among Divines may be thus abridg'd: It is so; It is not so; It is so; It is not so.
—BENJAMIN FRANKLIN, *Poor Richard's Almanack*, 1743

Men are extremely inclined to the passions of hope and fear; a religion, therefore, that has neither a heaven nor a hell could hardly please them.
—CHARLES DE MONTESQUIEU, *The Spirit of the Laws*, XXV, 2, 1748

Opposing one species of superstition to another, set them a quarreling; while we ourselves, during their fury and contention, happily make our escape into the calm, though obscure, regions of philosophy.
—DAVID HUME, *The Natural History of Religion*, 15, 1757

Shake off all the fears and servile prejudices under which weak minds are servilely crouched. Fix reason firmly in her seat, and call to her tribunal every fact, every opinion. Question with boldness even the existence of a god; because if there be one, he must more approve of the homage of reason, than that of blindfolded fear.
—THOMAS JEFFERSON, letter to Peter Carr (nephew), August 10, 1787

Religion

When men, whether from policy or pious fraud, set up systems of religion . . . they were under the necessity of inventing or adopting a word that should serve as a bar to all questions, inquiries and speculations. The word *mystery* answered this purpose; and thus it has happened that religion, which is in itself without mystery, has been corrupted into a fog of mysteries.
—THOMAS PAINE, *The Age of Reason*, I, 1794

I believe that religious duties consist in doing justice, loving mercy, and endeavoring to make our fellow creatures happy. . . . My own mind is my own church.
—THOMAS PAINE, *The Age of Reason*, I, 1794

I never told my own religion, nor scrutinized that of another. I never attempted to make a convert, nor wished to change another's creed. I have ever judged of others' religion by their lives. . . . For it is in our lives and not from our words, that our religion must be read.
—THOMAS JEFFERSON, letter to Mrs. Samuel H. Smith, August 6, 1816

To have a positive religion is not necessary. To be in harmony with oneself and the whole is what counts.
—JOHANN WOLFGANG VON GOETHE, Riemer's diaries (Weigand transl.), December 24, 1824

Religion may be defined thus: a belief in, and homage rendered to, existences unseen and causes unknown.
—FRANCES WRIGHT, *Course of Popular Lectures*, 5, 1829. Quoted in Gaylor, *Women Without Superstition* (1997)

Great Freethinkers

A sect or party is an elegant incognito devised to save man from the vexation of thinking.
—RALPH WALDO EMERSON, *Journals*, June 20, 1831

Man makes religion; religion does not make man.
—KARL MARX, "Critique of the Hegelian Philosophy of Right," *Deutsche-französische Yahrbücher*, 1844

For, as you know, religions are like glow-worms; they shine only when it's dark. A certain amount of general ignorance is the condition of all religions, the element in which alone they can exist.
—ARTHUR SCHOPENHAUER, *Parerga and Paralipomena*, Vol. II, 15, 1851

The entertaining a single thought of a certain elevation makes all men of one religion. It is always some base alloy that creates the distinction of sects. Thought greets thought over the widest gulfs of time with unerring freemasonry.
—HENRY DAVID THOREAU, *Journal*, August 8, 1852

Religion, although . . . preserv'd in the churches and creeds, does not depend at all upon them, but is a part of the identified soul, which . . . can really confront Religion when it extricates itself entirely from the churches, and not before.
—WALT WHITMAN, *Democratic Vistas*, 1871

At length I . . . found myself, with the last link of my chain snapped, a free rover on the broad, bright breezy common of the universe.
—HARRIET MARTINEAU, *Autobiography*, Vol. I, 1877. On her break with religion

Religion

Weariness that wants to reach the ultimate with one leap, with one fatal leap, a poor ignorant weariness that does not want to want any more: this created all gods and afterworlds.
—FRIEDRICH NIETZSCHE, *Thus Spoke Zarathustra* (Kaufmann transl.), I, 3, 1883

In religious history the import of a text is not what the author meant to say, but what the needs of the time made him say. The religious history of mankind is made up of mistranslations.
—JOSEPH ERNEST RENAN, *Histoire du peuple d'Israel*, Vol. IV, 1887-93. Quoted in Mott, *Ernest Renan* (1921)

Man is a religious animal. He is the only Religious animal. He is the only animal that has the True Religion – several of them. He is the only animal that loves his neighbor as himself and cuts his throat if his theology isn't straight.
—MARK TWAIN, *Letters from the Earth* (1962), "The Damned Human Race," ca. 1900

Religion remains an imaginative achievement, a symbolic represen-tation of moral reality which may have a most important function in vitalising the mind and in transmitting by way of parable, the lessons of experience. But it becomes at the same time a continuous incidental deception; and this deception, in proportion as it is stren-uously denied to be such, can work infinite harm in the world and in the conscience.
—GEORGE SANTAYANA, *Reason in Religion*, 1, 1905

If religions were got by reasoning, we should have the extraordinary spectacle of an American family with a Presbyterian in it, and a Baptist, a Methodist, a Catholic, a Mohammedan, a Buddhist, and

a Mormon. A Presbyterian family does not produce Catholic families or other religious brands, it produces its own kind; and not by intellectual processes, but by association.
—MARK TWAIN, *Christian Science*, 9, 1907

Intellectually, religious emotions are not creative but conservative. They attach themselves readily to the current view of the world and consecrate it.
—JOHN DEWEY, *The Influence of Darwin on Philosophy*, 1909

What is wrong with priests and popes is that instead of being apostles and saints, they are nothing but empirics who say "I know" instead of "I am learning," and pray for credulity and inertia as wise men pray for scepticism and activity.
—GEORGE BERNARD SHAW, *The Doctor's Dilemma*, "Preface," 1911

To sum up: 1. The cosmos is a gigantic fly-wheel making 10,000 revolutions a minute. 2. Man is a sick fly taking a dizzy ride on it. 3. Religion is the theory that the wheel was designed and set spinning to give him a ride.
—H. L. MENCKEN, "Coda," *Smart Set*, December 1920. Reprinted in *A Mencken Chrestomathy* (1949)

The more perfect the dogmatism, the more insecure. A great topsail that can never be reefed nor furled is the first carried away by the gale.
—GEORGE SANTAYANA, *Scepticism and Animal Faith*, 2, 1923

What would have been the effect upon religion if it had come to us through the minds of women? . . . Had the religions of the world developed through her mind, they would have shown one deep,

essential difference, the difference between birth and death. The man was interested in one end of life, she in the other. He was moved to faith, fear, and hope for the future; she to love and labor in the present.
—CHARLOTTE PERKINS GILMAN, *His Religion and Hers*, 3, 1923

To know that what is impenetrable to us really exists, manifesting itself as the highest wisdom and the most radiant beauty which our dull faculties can comprehend only in their most primitive forms – this knowledge, this feeling, is at the center of true religiousness. In this sense, and in this sense only, I belong in the ranks of devoutly religious men.
—ALBERT EINSTEIN, in Einstein et. al., *Living Philosophies*, 1931

If one attempts to assign to religion its place in man's evolution, it seems not so much to be a lasting acquisition, as a parallel to the neurosis which the civilized individual must pass through on his way from childhood to maturity.
—SIGMUND FREUD, *New Introductory Lectures on Psychoanalysis*, 7, 1933

It seems to me that organized creeds are collections of words around a wish. I feel no need for such. . . . The springing of the yellow line of morning out of the misty deep of dawn is glory enough for me.
—ZORA NEALE HURSTON, *Dust Tracks on a Road*, 15, 1942

Whether we are religionists or not, . . . we can unite in firm negation of idolatry and find perhaps more of a common faith in this negation than in any affirmative statements about God. Certainly we shall find more of humility and of brotherly love.
—ERICH FROMM, *Psychoanalysis and Religion*, 5, 1950

The idea of the sacred is quite simply one of the most conservative notions in any culture, because it seeks to turn other ideas – uncertainty, progress, change – into crimes.

—SALMAN RUSHDIE, *Is Nothing Sacred?* 1990

Tolerance is thin gruel compared to the rapture of absolute truths. It's not surprising that religious people are often better protected by atheists and agnostics than each other.

—WENDY KAMINER, "Absolutisms on Parade," *Free Inquiry*, Winter, 2001-02

Belief. Skepticism

Skepticism is an ability to place in opposition, in any manner whatever, appearances and judgements, and thus – because of the equality of force in the objects and arguments opposed – to come first of all to a suspension of judgement and then to mental tranquillity.

—SEXTUS EMPIRICUS, *Outline of Pyrrhonism*, I, 4 (Etheridge transl.), ca. 180 A.D.

Nothing is so firmly believed as that which is least known, nor are any people so confident as those who tell us fables, such as alchemists, seers, astrologers, palm-readers, doctors – that whole tribe. To whom I would add, if I dared, a whole pack of people, interpreters, and ordinary record keepers of God's designs.

—MICHEL DE MONTAIGNE, *Essays*, I, 32, 1580

Whatever is preached to us, whatever we learn, we should always remember that it is man that gives and man that receives; it is a mortal hand that offers it to us, a mortal hand that accepts it.
—MICHEL DE MONTAIGNE, *Essays*, II, 12, 1580

My interest in believing something is not a proof of its existence.
—VOLTAIRE, *Philosophical Letters*, 25, "On the Thoughts of Pascal," 1734

No testimony is sufficient to establish a miracle, unless the testimony be of such a kind, that its falsehood would be more miraculous than the fact which it endeavors to establish.
—DAVID HUME, *An Enquiry Concerning Human Understanding*, "Of Miracles," 1748

If reason is a gift from heaven, and if one can say the same about faith, then heaven has given us two incompatible and contradictory presents.
—DENIS DIDEROT, *Addition aux Pensées philosophiques*, 5, 1770

It is necessary to the happiness of man, that he be mentally faithful to himself. Infidelity does not consist in believing, or in disbelieving; it consists in professing to believe what he does not believe.
—THOMAS PAINE, *The Age of Reason*, I, 1794

It is a contradiction in terms and ideas, to call any thing a revelation that comes to us at second-hand, either verbally or in writing. Revelation is necessarily limited to the first communication – after this, it is only an account of something which that person says was a revelation made to him.
—THOMAS PAINE, *The Age of Reason*, I, 1794

A necessary consequent of religious belief is the attaching ideas of merit to that belief, and of demerit to its absence. Now here is a departure from the first principle of true ethics. Here we find ideas of moral wrong and moral right associated with something else than moral action.

—FRANCES WRIGHT, *Course of Popular Lectures*, "Lecture on Morals," 1829. Quoted in Gaylor, *Women Without Superstition* (1997)

The faith that stands on authority is not faith. The reliance on authority measures the decline of religion, the withdrawal of the soul.

—RALPH WALDO EMERSON, *Essays*, First Series, "The Over-Soul," 1841

A just thinker will allow full swing to his skepticism. I dip my pen in the blackest ink, because I am not afraid of falling into my inkpot.

—RALPH WALDO EMERSON, *The Conduct of Life*, "Worship," 1860

My business is to teach my aspirations to conform themselves to fact, not to try and make facts harmonize with my aspirations.

—THOMAS H. HUXLEY, Letter to Charles Kingsley, September 23, 1860. Quoted in *Life and Letters of Thomas Henry Huxley* (1900)

Religion attracts more devotion according as it demands more faith – that is to say, as it becomes more incredible to the profane mind. The philosopher aspires to explain away all mysteries, to dissolve them into light. Mystery on the other hand is demanded and pursued by the religious instinct; mystery constitutes the essence of worship.

—HENRI FRÉDÉRIC AMIEL, *Journal*, June 5, 1870

Religion

It is worthy of remark that a belief constantly inculcated during the early years of life, whilst the brain is impressible, appears to acquire almost the nature of an instinct; and the very essence of an instinct is that it is followed independently of reason.
—CHARLES DARWIN, *The Descent of Man*, 4, 1871

We are all tattooed in our cradles with the beliefs of our tribe.
—OLIVER WENDELL HOLMES, *The Poet at the Breakfast Table*, 1872

We should not let ourselves be burned at the stake for our opinions: we are not that sure of them. But perhaps for this: that we may have and change our opinions.
—FRIEDRICH NIETZSCHE, *The Wanderer and His Shadow*, 333, 1880

You are my believers; but of what account are all believers? You had not yet sought yourselves; then you found me. . . . Now I bid you lose me and find yourselves; and only when you have all denied me will I return to you.
—FRIEDRICH NIETZSCHE, Zarathustra in *Thus Spoke Zarathustra* (Kaufmann transl.), I, 22, 1883

To yearn for a strong faith is not the proof of a strong faith, but the reverse. If a man really have strong faith he can indulge in the beautiful luxury of skepticism. One is sure enough, strong enough, grounded enough for that.
—FRIEDRICH NIETZSCHE, *The Twilight of the Idols*, "Skirmishes of an Untimely Man," 12, 1889

I took thought, and invented what I conceived to be the appropriate title of "Agnostic." It came into my head as suggestively antithetic to the "Gnostic" of Church history who professed to know so much about the very things of which I was ignorant.
—THOMAS H. HUXLEY, *Collected Essays*, Vol. V, "Agnosticism," 1889

Reverence for one's own sacred things – parents, religion, flag, laws, and respect for one's own beliefs – these are feelings which we cannot even help. They come natural to us; they are involuntary, like breathing. There is no personal merit in breathing. But the reverence which is difficult, and which has personal merit in it, is the respect which you pay, without compulsion, to the political or religious attitude of a man whose beliefs are not yours.
—MARK TWAIN, *Following the Equator*, Vol. II, 17, 1897

It was a schoolboy who said: "Faith is believing what you know ain't so."
—MARK TWAIN, *Following the Equator*, Vol. I, 12, "Pudd'nhead Wilson's New Calendar," 1897

It is perhaps not surprising that men come to regard the happiness which a religious belief affords as a proof of its truth. If a creed makes a man feel happy, he almost inevitably adopts it. Such a belief ought to be true; therefore it is true.
—WILLIAM JAMES, *The Varieties of Religious Experience*, 4 & 5, 1902

Skepticism, instead of seeming, what it naturally is, a moral force, a tendency to sincerity, economy, and fine adjustment of life and mind to experience – skepticism seemed a temptation and a danger. This

situation, which still prevails in a certain measure, strikingly shows into how artificial a posture Christianity has thrown the mind.
—GEORGE SANTAYANA, *Reason in Religion*, 7, 1905

The fact that a believer is happier than a skeptic is no more to the point than the fact that a drunken man is happier than a sober one. The happiness of credulity is a cheap and dangerous quality of happiness, and by no means a necessity of life.
—GEORGE BERNARD SHAW, *Androcles and the Lion*, "Preface," 1912

I am convinced that if a dozen skeptics were to draw up in parallel columns a list of the events narrated in the gospels which they consider credible and incredible respectively, their lists would be different in several particulars. Belief is literally a matter of taste.
—GEORGE BERNARD SHAW, *Androcles and the Lion*, "Preface," 1912

The natural tendency of man is not to press home a doubt, but to cut inquiry as short as possible. The practical man's impatience with theory has become a proverb; it expresses just the feeling that, since the thinking process is of use only in substituting certainty for doubt, any apparent prolongation of it is useless speculation, wasting time and diverting the mind from important issues.
—JOHN DEWEY, *Essays in Experimental Logic*, 6, 1916

Despite the common delusion to the contrary the philosophy of doubt is far more comforting than that of hope. The doubter escapes the worst penalty of the man of faith and hope; he is never disappointed, and hence never indignant.
—H. L. MENCKEN, *Damn! A Book of Calumny*, 43, 1918

Great Freethinkers

Skepticism! This word is made synonymous with negation and impotence. Yet, our great skeptics were sometimes the most affirmative, and often the most courageous, of men. They denied only negations. They attacked everything that fetters the mind and the will.
—ANATOLE FRANCE, *The Opinions of Anatole France*, "The Credo of a Skeptic," 1921

No matter what the belief, if it had modestly said, "This is our best thought, go on, think farther!" then we could have smoothly outgrown our early errors and long since have developed a religion such as would have kept pace with an advancing world. But we were made to believe and not allowed to think. We were told to obey, rather than to experiment and investigate.
—CHARLOTTE PERKINS GILMAN, *His Religion and Hers*, 1923. Quoted in Gaylor, *Women without Superstition* (1997)

We call a belief an illusion when wish-fulfillment is a prominent factor in its motivation, irregardless of its relation to reality.
—SIGMUND FREUD, *The Future of an Illusion*, 6, 1927

The devout believer is in a high degree protected against the danger of certain neurotic afflictions; by accepting the universal neurosis, he is spared the task of forming a personal one.
—SIGMUND FREUD, *The Future of an Illusion*, 8, 1927

One can only believe entirely, perhaps, in what one cannot see.
—VIRGINIA WOOLF, *Orlando*, 1928

Religion

One cannot order one's life without a set of beliefs of some kind. But the intellectually honest man must recognize the utterly provisional nature of his beliefs.

—J. B. S. HALDANE, *The Inequality of Man and Other Essays*, "My Philosophy of Life," 1932

To teach how to live without certainty, and yet without being paralyzed by hesitation, is perhaps the chief thing that philosophy, in our age, can still do for those who study it.

—BERTRAND RUSSELL, *History of Western Philosophy*, "Introduction," 1945

As a set of cognitive beliefs, religion is a speculative hypothesis of an extremely low order of probability.

—SIDNEY HOOK, "Religion and the Intellectuals," *Partisan Review*, March, 1950

The opposite of the religious fanatic is not the fanatical atheist but the gentle cynic who cares not whether there is a God or not.

—ERIC HOFFER, *The True Believer*, 3, 1951

In its more authoritarian forms, religion punishes questioning and rewards gullibility. Faith is not a function of stupidity, but a frequent cause of it.

—WENDY KAMINER, "The Last Taboo," *The New Republic*, October 14, 1996

Deity

Aethiopians have gods with snub noses and black hair, Thracians have gods with grey eyes and red hair.
—XENOPHANES, Fragments (Freeman transl.), 6th century B.C.

Men are bound to believe in some ruler or rulers of the universe . . . who have arranged and adapted everything for human use. They are bound to estimate the nature of such rulers – having no information on the subject – in accordance with their own nature, and therefore they assert that the gods ordained everything for the use of man in order to bind man to themselves and obtain from him the highest honour.
—BENEDICT DE SPINOZA, *Ethics*, I, "Appendix," 1677

I imagine it great Vanity in me to suppose, that the *Supremely Perfect* does in the least regard such an inconsiderable Nothing as Man. More especially, since it is impossible for me to have any positive clear Idea of that which is infinite and incomprehensible, I cannot conceive otherwise, than that He, *the Infinite Father*, expects or requires no Worship or Praise from us, but that he is even Infinitely Above It.
—BENJAMIN FRANKLIN, *Articles of Belief and Acts of Religion*, 1728

If God made us in his image, we have more than returned the favor.
—VOLTAIRE, *Le Sottisier*, mid-18th century

In general believers fashion God after themselves; the good make him good, the wicked make him wicked.
—JEAN-JACQUES ROUSSEAU, *The Confessions*, VI, 1782

For my part, I cannot be satisfied with one way of thinking. As a poet and artist, I am a polytheist; in my scientific studies I am a pantheist. . . . When I feel a personal need for one god in my ethical life, this is taken care of as well.

—JOHANN WOLFGANG VON GOETHE, letter to F. Jacobi, January 6, 1813

Such as are a man's thoughts and dispositions, such is his God; so much worth as a man has, so much and no more has his God. Consciousness of God is self-consciousness; knowledge of God is self-knowledge.

—LUDWIG FEUERBACH, *The Essence of Christianity*, I, 2, 1840

In the face of our misery and want we are charged twenty millions for the worship of God [in taxes to support the Anglican Church]. . . . If poor men cost the state so much, they would be put like officers on half-pay. I think that while our own distress lasts it would be wise to do the same with the deity.

—GEORGE HOLYOAKE, speech at Cheltenham on May 24, 1842. Quoted in MacCabe, *Life and Letters of G.J. Holyoake*. On the basis of these words Holyoake was imprisoned for six months for blasphemy.

The more man puts into God, the less he retains in himself.

—KARL MARX, *Economic and Philosophic Manuscripts* (1932), 1844

In my Pantheon, Pan still reigns in his pristine glory, with his ruddy face, his flowing beard, and his shaggy body, his pipe and his crook, his nymph Echo, and his chosen daughter Iambe; for the great god Pan is not dead, as was rumored. No god ever dies. Perhaps of all the gods of New England and of ancient Greece, I am most constant at his shrine.

—HENRY DAVID THOREAU, *A Week on the Concord and Merrimack Rivers*, "Sunday," 1849

We need pray for no higher heaven than the pure senses can furnish, a *purely* sensuous life. . . . May we not *see* God? Are we to be put off and amused in this life, as it were with a mere allegory?
—HENRY DAVID THOREAU, *A Week on the Concord and Merrimack Rivers*, "Friday," 1849

God is the sole being who, in order to rule, does not even need to exist.
—CHARLES BAUDELAIRE, *Journaux intimes*, "Fusées," 1, mid-19th century

It is only to monotheism that intolerance is essential; an only god is by his nature a jealous god, who can allow no other god to exist.
—ARTHUR SCHOPENHAUER, *Parerga and Paralipomena*, Vol. II, 15, 1851

The manner in which all the religions talk of God, the way they treat him with certainty, frivolity, and familiarity, disgusts me. The priests, who have his name always on the tip of their tongues, are especially irritating. It is a kind of sneezing which is habitual for them: "The goodness of God," "the wrath of God," "offending God," these are the words they use. It is treating him like a man, and even worse, a bourgeois.
—GUSTAVE FLAUBERT, letter to Mme. Roger des Genettes, 1859-60

I did not know we had ever quarrelled, Aunt.
—HENRY DAVID THOREAU, words prior to death in answer to his aunt's question "Have you made your peace with God?" Reported in Edward W. Emerson, *Henry Thoreau as Remembered by a Young Friend* (1917), 1862

The atheist does not say, "There is no God," but he says, "I know not what you mean by God; the very word God is to me a sound conveying no clear or distinct affirmation."
—CHARLES BRADLAUGH, *A Plea for Atheism*, 1864

All the emotion we can possibly possess, all the feeling of which human nature is capable, all belongs to man. If there be one God or ten thousand gods, they do not need it, but man does and woman does, and to me it is stealing from man what belongs to man to give to a god.
—ERNESTINE L. ROSE, speech delivered in London at the General Conference of Liberal Thinkers, June, 1878. Quoted in Gaylor, *Women Without Superstition* (1997)

Do we not hear the noise of the gravediggers who are burying God? Do we not smell the divine putrefaction? – for even Gods putrefy. God is dead. God remains dead. And we have killed him.
—FRIEDRICH NIETZSCHE, *The Gay Science*, 125, 1882

I would only believe in a God who knew how to dance.
—FRIEDRICH NIETZSCHE, *Thus Spoke Zarathustra*, I, 7, 1883

I distrust those people who know so well what God wants them to do because I notice it always coincides with their own desires.
—SUSAN B. ANTHONY, remarks to National American Woman Suffrage Association, January 23-26, 1896. Quoted in Stanton et. al., *History of Woman Suffrage*, Vol. IV, 16

If I were going to construct a God I would furnish Him with some ways and qualities and characteristics which the Present (Bible) One lacks. He would not stoop to *ask* for any man's compliments, praises, flatteries; and He would be far above *exacting* them. I would have Him as self-respecting as the better sort of man in these regards.

—MARK TWAIN, *Mark Twain's Notebook* (1935), June 18, 1896

What God lacks is convictions – stability of character. He ought to be a Presbyterian or a Catholic or *something* – not try to be everything.

— MARK TWAIN, *Mark Twain's Notebook* (1935), Summer, 1898

We arrive at the paradoxical conception of God as a *gaseous vertebrate.*

—ERNST HAECKEL, *The Riddle of the Universe*, 15, 1899

God and the devil are an effort after specialisation and division of labour.

—SAMUEL BUTLER, *Notebooks* (1912), 14, late 19th century

Theist and Atheist. The fight between them is as to whether God shall be called God or shall have some other name.

—SAMUEL BUTLER, *Note-Books* (1912), 21, late 19th century

The gods we stand by are the gods we need and can use, the gods whose demands on us are reinforcements of our demands on ourselves and on one another.

—WILLIAM JAMES, *The Varieties of Religious Experience*, 14 & 15, 1902

Few historic changes are more curious than these mutations of theological opinion. The monarchical type of sovereignty was, for example, so ineradicably planted in the minds of our own forefathers that a dose of cruelty and arbitrariness in their deity seems positively to have been required by their imagination. . . . But today we abhor the very notion of eternal suffering inflicted.
—WILLIAM JAMES, *The Varieties of Religious Experience*, 14 & 15, 1902

We are told that when Jehovah created the world he saw that it was good. What would he say now?
—GEORGE BERNARD SHAW, *Man and Superman*, "Maxims for Revolutionists," 1903

The thoughts of the gods are no less changeable than those of the men who interpret them. They advance, but they always lag behind the thoughts of men. . . . The Christian God was once a Jew. Now he is an anti-Semite.
—ANATOLE FRANCE, letter to Freethought Congress, 1905. Quoted in McCabe, *A Biographical Dictionary of Modern Rationalists* (1920)

It is pathetic to observe how lowly the motives are that religion, even the highest, attributes to the deity. . . . To be given the best morsel, to be remembered, to be praised, to be obeyed blindly and punctiliously – these have been thought points of honor with the gods.
—GEORGE SANTAYANA, *Reason in Religion*, 3, 1905

The scale of the evil actually in sight defies all human tolerance. . . . A God who can relish such superfluities of horror is no God for

human beings to appeal to. His animal spirits are too high. In other words, the 'Absolute' with his one purpose, is not the manlike God of common people.
—WILLIAM JAMES, *Pragmatism*, 1907

It has been said that the greatest praise of God lies in the negation of the atheist, who considers creation sufficiently perfect to dispense with the creator.
—MARCEL PROUST, *Le côté de Guermantes*, 1921

My atheism, like that of Spinoza, is true piety towards the universe and denies only gods fashioned by men in their own image, to be servants of their human interests; and that even in this denial I am no rude iconoclast, but full of secret sympathy with the impulses of idolaters.
—GEORGE SANTAYANA, *Soliloquies in England and Later Soliloquies*, 54, 1922

The world-old notion of a creator and director, sitting apart from the universe and shaping and controlling its affairs, a magnified king or emperor, finds no lodgment in my mind. Kings and despots have had their day, both in heaven and on earth. The universe is a democracy.
—JOHN BURROUGHS, *The Last Harvest*, "A Critical Glance into Darwin," 1922

I cannot imagine a God who rewards and punishes the objects of his creation, whose purposes are modeled after our own – a God, in short, who is but a reflection of human frailty. . . . It is enough for me to contemplate the mystery of conscious life perpetuating itself through all eternity.
—ALBERT EINSTEIN, statement in Einstein et. al., *Living Philosophies*, 1931

So long as, on the one hand, scientific knowledge is preserved and expanded, and on the other, man keeps his ethical standards above those of nature, the prospects for god-makers are by no means as rosy as they were in the past.
—J. B. S. HALDANE, *The Inequality of Man and Other Essays*, "God-Makers," 1932

Our nada who art in nada, nada be thy name. Thy kingdom nada, thy will be nada as it is in nada. Give us this nada our daily nada and nada us our nada as we nada our nadas and nada us into nada but deliver us from nada.
—ERNEST HEMINGWAY, *Winner Take Nothing*, "A Clean Well-Lighted Place," 1933

To imagine that we are going to be saved by outside intervention, whether in the shape of an analyst, a dictator, a savior, or even a God, is sheer folly. There are not enough lifeboats to go around, and anyway . . . what is needed more than lifeboats is lighthouses. A fuller, clearer vision – not more safety appliances.
—HENRY MILLER, *The Wisdom of the Heart*, 1941

It is because men, far from being granted a total license by the absence of God, are abandonned on earth that their acts become definite, absolute commitments.
—SIMONE DE BEAUVOIR, *The Ethics of Ambiguity*, 1, 1948

If you are going to stress the enormous transcendence of God you are – to put it gently – in danger of undermining the possibility of saying anything intelligible about him.
—ANTONY FLEW, *New Essays in Philosophical Theology*, "Creation," 1955

Monotheistic religions themselves have, to a large extent, regressed into idolatry. Man projects his power of love and of reason unto God; he does not feel them any more as his own powers, and then he prays to God to give him back some of what he, man, has projected unto God.
— ERICH FROMM, *The Sane Society*, V, 1955

It is impossible to imagine the universe run by a wise, just, and omnipotent God, but it is quite easy to imagine it run by a board of gods. If such a board actually exists it operates precisely like the board of a corporation that is losing money.
—H. L. MENCKEN, *Minority Report*, 79, 1956

God and Satan alike are essentially human figures, the one a projection of ourselves, the other of our enemies.
—BERTRAND RUSSELL, *Understanding Human History*, "The Value of Free Thought," 1957

We are all atheists about most of the gods humanity has ever believed in – some of us just go one god further.
—RICHARD DAWKINS, "A Challenge to Atheists," *Free Inquiry*, summer, 2002

Morality

One might perhaps expect gnawings of conscience and repentance to help bring men on the right path, and might thereupon conclude . . . that these affections are good things. Yet when we look at the

matter closely, we shall find that they are not only not good, but on the contrary, deleterious and evil passions. We can always get along better by reason and love of truth than by worry of conscience and remorse.
—BENEDICT DE SPINOZA, *Tract on God, Man, and Happiness*, II, 10, ca. 1662

Superstitious persons, who know better how to rail at vice than how to teach virtue, and who strive not to guide men by reason but to so restrain them that they would rather escape evil than love virtue, aim only to make others as wretched as themselves.
—BENEDICT DE SPINOZA, *Ethics*, IV, 63, 1677

Improvement in Religion is called *Building Up* and *Edification*. *Faith* is then the Ground-floor, *Hope* is up one Pair of Stairs. My dear beloved Jenny, don't delight so much to dwell in these lower Rooms, but get as fast as you can into the Garret; for in truth the best Room in the House is *Charity*.
—BENJAMIN FRANKLIN, letter to Jane Mecom, September 16, 1758

The law of doing good is drawn from reason; and the Christian needs only logic to be virtuous.
—JEAN-JACQUES ROUSSEAU, letter to M. d'Offreville, October 4, 1761

The commandments carry no internal evidence of divinity with them; they contain some good moral precepts, such as any man qualified to be a lawgiver, or a legislator, could produce himself, without having recourse to supernatural intervention.
—THOMAS PAINE, *The Age of Reason*, I, 1794

I believe that the error of religionists lies in this, that they do not know the extent or the harmony or the depth of their moral nature; that they are clinging to little, positive, verbal, formal versions of the moral law, and very imperfect versions too, while the infinite laws, the laws of the Law . . . are all unobserved.
—RALPH WALDO EMERSON, *Journals*, Sept. 8, 1833

The theological problems of original sin, origin of evil, predestination, and the like are the soul's mumps, and measles, and whooping coughs.
—RALPH WALDO EMERSON, *Essays*, First Series, "Spiritual Laws," 1841

Do not be too moral. You may cheat yourself out of much life so. Aim above morality. Be not simply good, be good for something.
—HENRY DAVID THOREAU, letter to Mr. B., March 7, 1848

Christian morality (so called) has all the characters of a reaction; it is, in great part, a protest against Paganism. Its ideal is negative rather than positive; passive rather than active; Innocence rather than Nobleness; Abstinence from Evil, rather than energetic Pursuit of Good: in its precepts (as has been well said) "thou shalt not" predominates unduly over "thou shalt". . . . It is essentially a doctrine of passive obedience.
—JOHN STUART MILL, *On Liberty*, 2, 1859

Whatever good you would do out of fear of punishment, or hope of reward hereafter, the Atheist would do simply because it is good; and being so, he would receive the far surer and more certain reward, springing from well-doing, which would constitute his pleasure, and promote his happiness.
—ERNESTINE L. ROSE, "A Defence of Atheism," lecture in Boston, April 10, 1861. Quoted in Gaylor, *Women Without Superstition* (1997)

Freedom, morality, and the human dignity of the individual consists precisely in this: that he does good not because he is forced to do so, but because he freely conceives it, wants it, and loves it.
—MIKHAIL BAKUNIN, *God and the State*, 1871

That altruism is right but that egoism is also right, and that there requires a continual compromise between the two, is a conclusion which few consciously formulate, and fewer avow.
—HERBERT SPENCER, *The Study of Sociology*, 8, 1873

There is a very real evil consequent on ascribing a supernatural origin to the received maxims of morality. That origin consecrates the whole of them, and protects them from being discussed or criticized.
—JOHN STUART MILL, *Three Essays on Religion*, "Utility of Religion," 1874

The religions which deal in promises and threats regarding a future life . . . fasten down the thoughts to the person's own posthumous interests; they tempt him to regard the performance of his duties to others mainly as a means to his own personal salvation; and are one of the most serious obstacles to the great purpose of moral culture, the strengthening of the unselfish and weakening of the selfish element in our nature.
—JOHN STUART MILL, *Three Essays on Religion*, "Utility of Religion," 1874

Kindness, friendliness, the courtesy of the heart . . . have been of far greater help to culture than those much more famous manifestations called pity, compassion, and self-sacrifice.
—FRIEDRICH NIETZSCHE, *Human All Too Human*, 49, 1878

Submission to morality can be slavish or vain or selfish or resigned or obtusely enthusiastic or thoughtless or an act of desperation, like submission to a prince: in itself it is nothing moral.
—FRIEDRICH NIETZSCHE, *Dawn* (Kaufmann transl.), 97, 1881

If you have an enemy, do not requite him evil with good, for that would put him to shame. Rather prove that he did you some good.
—FRIEDRICH NIETZSCHE, *Thus Spoke Zarathustra* (Kaufmann transl.), I, 19, 1883

Would that you might invent for me the love that bears not only all punishment but also all guilt!
—FRIEDRICH NIETZSCHE, *Thus Spoke Zarathustra* (Kaufmann transl.), I, 19, 1883

To attain individual morality in an age demanding social morality, to pride one's self on the results of personal effort when the time demands social adjustment, is utterly to fail to apprehend the situation.
—JANE ADDAMS, *Democracy and Social Ethics*, "Democracy and Social Ethics," 1902

The seven deadly sins. . . . Food, clothing, firing, rent, taxes, respectability, and children. Nothing can lift those seven millstones from man's neck but money; and the spirit cannot soar until the millstones are lifted.
—GEORGE BERNARD SHAW, *Major Barbara*, III, 1907

"Blessed are the meek, for they shall inherit the earth." What a preposterous notion! What incentive to slavery, inactivity, and para-

sitism! Besides, it is not true that the meek can inherit anything. Just because humanity has been meek, the earth has been stolen from it.
—EMMA GOLDMAN, "The Failure of Christianity," *Mother Earth*, April, 1913

The puritan . . . gets the satisfaction of his will to power through the turning of his self-abasement into purposes of self-regard. Renunciation is the raw material for his positive sense of power.
—RANDOLPH BOURNE, *The History of a Literary Radical*, "The Puritan's Will to Power," 1920

Most of us . . . after we have had our puritan fling, sown our puritan wild oats as it were, grow up into devout and progressing pagans, cultivating the warmth of the sun, the deliciousness of love-experience, the high moods of art. The puritans remain around us, a danger and a threat. But they have value to us in keeping us acutely self-conscious of our faith. They whet our ardor. Perhaps no one can be really a good appreciating pagan who has not once been a bad puritan.
—RANDOLPH BOURNE, *The History of a Literary Radical*, "The Puritan's Will to Power," 1920

The Churches must learn humility as well as teach it.
—GEORGE BERNARD SHAW, *Saint Joan*, "Preface," 1924

Morality is of the highest importance – but for us, not for God.
—ALBERT EINSTEIN, letter to a banker in Colorado, August, 1927. Quoted in Dukas & Hoffmann, *Albert Einstein: The Human Side* (1979)

There exists a clear distinction between a morality of obedience and a morality of attachment or reciprocity, and the latter is the morality of harmonious societies.
—HERBERT READ, *Education Through Art*, 1943

Every neurosis represents a moral problem. The failure to achieve maturity and integration of the whole personality is a moral problem.
—ERICH FROMM, *Man for Himself*, IV, 5, 1947

Guilt feelings have proved to be the most effective means of forming and increasing dependency, and herein lies one of the social functions of authoritarian ethics throughout society.
—ERICH FROMM, *Man for Himself*, IV, 2, 1947

There is perhaps no phenomenon which contains so much destructive feeling as "moral indignation," which permits envy or hate to be acted out under the guise of virtue.
—ERICH FROMM, *Man for Himself*, IV, 5, 1947

No one can be good for long if goodness is not in demand.
—BERTOLT BRECHT, First God in *The Good Woman of Setzuan*, 1a, 1953

All human progress, even in morals, has been the work of men who have doubted the current moral values, not of men who have whooped them up and tried to enforce them. The truly civilized man is always skeptical and tolerant.
—H. L. MENCKEN, *Minority Report*, 418, 1956

Those who are interested . . . will have to decide, upon the evidence, for themselves whether their goodness is to be their religion or whether

their religion is to be their goodness. Whether God is love, or whether love is God. Whether we will continue to suspend our gods in the heavens or whether we shall be willing to bring them down to earth.
—ASHLEY MONTAGU, *Man Observed*, 12, 1968

We are not so good, as a species, to be human*ists* with a chauvinistic inflection. None of us has a claim to a "morality" – left or right, atheist or theist – which exudes self-righteousness and absolutism.
—BARBARA EHRENREICH, "U.S. Patriots: Without God on their Side," *Mother Jones*, February/March, 1981

The greatest tragedy in mankind's entire history may be the hijacking of morality by religion.
—ARTHUR C. CLARKE, "Credo," in Clifton Fadiman, ed., *Living Philosophies*, 1991

Soul. Immortality

Till you know about the living, how are you to know about the dead?
—CONFUCIUS, *Analects* (Waley transl.), XI, 11, 6th-5th Century B.C.

It naturally follows then that the whole nature of the soul is dissolved, like smoke, into the high air, since we see it is begotten along with the body and grows up along with it and . . . breaks down at the same time, worn out with age.
—LUCRETIUS, *On the Nature of Things*, III, ca. 50 B.C.

They who would disunite our two principal parts, and isolate them from one another, are mistaken. On the contrary, we must recouple them and rejoin them. We must bid the soul not to draw aside and maintain herself apart, not to despise and desert the body . . . but to connect herself with it, embrace it, cherish it.
—MICHEL DE MONTAIGNE, *Essays* (Ives transl.), II, 17, 1580

Now upon *Death*, and the Destruction of the Body, the Ideas contain'd in the Brain . . . being then likewise necessarily destroy'd, the Soul, tho' incapable of Destruction itself, must then necessarily *cease to think* or *act*, having nothing left to think or act upon. It is reduc'd to its first inconscious State before it receiv'd any Ideas. And to cease to *think* is but little different from *ceasing to be*.
—BENJAMIN FRANKLIN, *A Dissertation on Liberty and Necessity, Pleasure and Pain*, 1725

All Bibles or sacred codes have been the causes of the following Errors. 1. That Man has two real existing principles Viz: a Body & a Soul. 2. That Energy called Evil is alone from the Body & that Reason called Good is alone from the Soul. 3. That God will torment Man in Eternity for following his Energies.
—WILLIAM BLAKE, *Marriage of Heaven and Hell*, 1793

If the philosopher tries to deduce the immortality of the soul from a legend, it means little. To me, the eternal existence of my soul is proved from my idea of activity; if I work on incessantly till my death, nature is bound to give me another form of existence when the present one can no longer sustain my spirit.
— JOHANN WOLFGANG VON GOETHE, *Conversations with Eckermann* (1836), February 4, 1829

Our life is but the Soul made known by its fruits, the body. The whole duty of man may be expressed in one line: Make to yourself a perfect body.
—HENRY DAVID THOREAU, *Journal*, June 21, 1840

How earthy old people become, – mouldy as the grave! Their wisdom smacks of the earth. There is no foretaste of immortality in it.
—HENRY DAVID THOREAU, *Journal*, August 16, 1853

Of immortality, the soul, when well employed, is incurious. It is so well, that it is sure it will be well. It asks no questions of the Supreme Power.
—RALPH WALDO EMERSON, *The Conduct of Life*, "Worship," 1860

The soul itself sits on a throne of nucleated cells, and flashes its mandates through skeins of glassy filaments.
—OLIVER WENDELL HOLMES, *Border Lines of Knowledge in Some Provinces of Medical Science*, 1862

It seems to me . . . that human nature, though pleased with the present, and by no means impatient to quit it, would find comfort and not sadness in the thought that it is not chained through eternity to a conscious existence which it cannot be assured that it will always wish to preserve.
— JOHN STUART MILL, *Three Essays on Religion*, "Utility of Religion," 1874

The certain prospect of death could sweeten every life with a precious and fragrant drop of levity – and now you strange apothecary souls have turned it into an ill-tasting drop of poison that makes the whole of life repulsive.

—FRIEDRICH NIETZSCHE, *The Wanderer and His Shadow*, 322, 1880

Nature holds her secret well-enveloped – as you put it, *her palm is closed*. . . . If immortality is right, we will have it – indeed, have it not alone but along with many other things undreamed of in our fighting philosophies; if *not* right, then *no* immortality.

—WALT WHITMAN, quoted in Traubel, *Walt Whitman in Camden*, Vol. IX, December 2, 1891. Whitman's last recorded comments on the subject of immortality

I used to sit for hours by her grave, and it was impossible for me then, as it is impossible for me now, to accept the ordinary doctrine that she was living somewhere without a body. . . . The whole of existence seemed to me more beautiful because it had brought forth and taken back to itself such a beautiful thing as she was to me.

—OLIVE SCHREINER, letter to John Lloyd, October 29, 1892. Quoted in Cronwright-Schreiner, *The Life of Olive Schreiner*. On the death of her favorite sister in childhood

The fact of having been born is a very bad augury for immortality.

—GEORGE SANTAYANA, *Reason in Religion*, 13, 1905

Our own death is indeed unimaginable, and whenever we make the attempt to imagine it we can perceive that we really survive as spectators. . . . In the unconscious every one of us is convinced of his own immortality.

—SIGMUND FREUD, "Thoughts for the Times on War and Death," *Imago*, 5, 1915

Religion

Since our inner experiences consist of reproductions and combinations of sensory impressions, the concept of a soul without a body seems to be empty and devoid of meaning.
—ALBERT EINSTEIN, letter to a Viennese woman, February 5, 1921. Quoted in Dukas & Hoffmann, *Albert Einstein: The Human Side* (1979)

The death-based religions have led to a limitless individualism, a demand for the eternal extension of personality.
—CHARLOTTE PERKINS GILMAN, *His Religion and Hers*, 3, 1923. Quoted in Gaylor, *Women without Superstition* (1997)

If only religion could be brought to take an interest in this earthly future, what a help it would be! . . . Think of the appeal to the less spiritual of us, to those who never did get enthusiastic about eternity, or care so tenderly about their own souls, yet who could rise to the thought of improving this world for the children they love, and their children after them.
— CHARLOTTE PERKINS GILMAN, *His Religion and Hers*, 2, 1923

The individual life of the larger animals, the soma, is a sacrifice of physical immortality in exchange for power and achievement. The individual has, so to speak, made a bargain. For the individual comes out of the germ-plasm and does and lives and at length dies for the sake of life. . . . A bacterium, as we have shown, is *all* germ-plasm, all reproductive material, and there is no soma to die. But its activities are very limited.
— H. G. WELLS, *The Science of Life*, IV, 5, 1929

The history of our era is the nauseating and repulsive history of the crucifixion of the procreative body for the glorification of the spirit,

the mental consciousness. Plato was an arch-priest of this cruci-fixion.
—D. H. LAWRENCE, *The Painting of D. H. Lawrence*, "Introduction to these Paintings," 1929

Immortality, as they [theologians] preach it in the modern world, is little more than a handy device for giving force and effect to their system of transcendental jurisprudence: what it amounts to is simply a threat that the contumacious will not be able to escape them by dying.
—H. L. MENCKEN, *Treatise on the Gods*, 1, 1930

The living self. . . . is not *spirit*. Spirit is merely our mental consciousness, a finished essence extracted from our life-being, just as alcohol, spirits of wine, is the material, finished essence extracted from the living grape.
—D. H. LAWRENCE, *Phoenix*, "Democracy," 1936

Who the hell should care about saving his soul when it is a man's duty to lose it intelligently, the way you would sell a position you were defending, if you could not hold it, as expensively as possible.
—ERNEST HEMINGWAY, quoted in Ross, *Portrait of Hemingway* (1961), mid 20th century

I believe in life everlasting; but not for the individual.
—GEORGE BERNARD SHAW, statement on his death bed, October 25, 1950, in Lawrence, ed., *Collected Letters*, Vol. IV

Psychology
&
Experience

Human Nature

All contradictions can be found in me at some moment and in some fashion. Bashful, insolent; chaste, licentious; talkative, taciturn; rough, gentle; clever, stupid; disagreeable, affable; lying, truthful; learned, ignorant; liberal, avaricious, and prodigal. . . . I can say nothing of myself absolutely, simply, and solidly, without confusion and mixture, nor in one word.
—MICHEL DE MONTAIGNE, *Essays*, II, 1, 1580

I put for a general inclination of all mankind a perpetual and restless desire of power after power that ceases only in death. And the cause of this is . . . because he cannot assure the power and means to live well which he has present without the acquisition of more.
—THOMAS HOBBES, *Leviathan*, I, 11, 1651

How selfish soever man may be supposed, there are evidently some principles in his nature which interest him in the fortunes of others and render their happiness necessary to him, though he derives nothing from it, except the pleasure of seeing it. Of this kind is pity or compassion, the emotion which we feel for the misery of others. . . . The greatest ruffian, the most hardened violator of the laws of society, is not altogether without it.

—ADAM SMITH, *The Theory of Moral Sentiments*, I, 1, 1, 1759

Let us lay it down as an incontestible maxim that the first promptings of nature are always right. There is no original corruption in the human heart: there is not a single vice to be found there of which one could not say how and by what means it entered.

—JEAN-JACQUES ROUSSEAU, *Émile*, II, 1762

Men I find to be a Sort of Beings very badly constructed, as they are generally more easily provok'd than reconcil'd, more disposed to do Mischief to each other than to make Reparation, much more easily deceiv'd than undeceiv'd, and having more Pride and even Pleasure in killing than in begetting one another.

—BENJAMIN FRANKLIN, letter to Joseph Priestley, June 7, 1782

The moral sense, or conscience, is as much a part of man as his leg or arm. It is given to all human beings in a stronger or weaker degree. . . . It may be strengthened by exercise, as may any particular limb of the body.

—THOMAS JEFFERSON, letter to Peter Carr, August 10, 1787

Mankind? That is an abstraction. It has always been only individuals who exist, and it will never be otherwise.

—JOHANN WOLFGANG VON GOETHE, conversation with Luden (Weigand transl.), August 19, 1806

As we are constituted by nature, there is not a fault that could not turn into a virtue, and not a virtue that could not turn into a fault.
—JOHANN WOLFGANG VON GOETHE, *Wilhelm Meister's Journeyings*, 1, 10, 1829

The doctor sees all the weakness of mankind, the lawyer all the wickedness, the theologian all the stupidity.
—ARTHUR SCHOPENHAUER, *Parerga and Paralipomena*, Vol. II, 26, 1851

The civilized man is a more experienced and wiser savage.
— HENRY DAVID THOREAU, *Walden*, "Economy," 1854

The social instincts, which no doubt were acquired by man as by the lower animals for the good of the community, will from the first have given to him some wish to aid his fellows, some feeling of sympathy, and have compelled him to regard their approbation and disapprobation. Such impulses will have served him at a very early period as a rude rule of right and wrong.
—CHARLES DARWIN, *The Descent of Man*, 4, 1871

Man, relatively speaking, is the most botched of all the animals and the sickliest, and he has wandered the most dangerously from his instincts.
—FRIEDRICH NIETZSCHE, *The Antichrist*, 14, 1888

Disobedience, in the eyes of any one who has read history, is man's original virtue. It is through disobedience that progress has been made, through disobedience and rebellion.
—OSCAR WILDE, "The Soul of Man under Socialism," *Fortnightly Review*, February, 1891

Men, my dear, are very queer animals, a mixture of horse-nervousness, ass-stubbornness, and camel-malice, with an angel bobbing about unexpectedly in the posset, and when they can do exactly as they please, they are very hard to drive.

— THOMAS HUXLEY, letter to Mrs. W.K. Clifford, February 10, 1895

Man is the Only Animal that Blushes. Or needs to.

—MARK TWAIN, *Following the Equator*, Vol. I, 27, "Pudd'nhead Wilson's New Calendar," 1897

Man, biologically considered, . . . is the most formidable of all beasts of prey, and, indeed, the only one that preys systematically on its own species.

—WILLIAM JAMES, *Memories and Studies* (1911), "Remarks at the Peace Banquet," 1904

The inmost essence of human nature consists of elemental instincts, which are common to all men and aim at the satisfaction of primal needs. These instincts in themselves are neither good nor evil. We but classify them and their manifestations in that fashion according as they meet the needs and demands of the human community.

—SIGMUND FREUD, "Thoughts for the Times on War and Death," *Imago*, 5, 1915

And now, it seems to me, the meaning of the evolution of culture is no longer a riddle to us. It must present to us the struggle between Eros and Death, between the instincts of life and the instincts of destruction, as it works itself out in the human species.

—SIGMUND FREUD, *Civilization and its Discontents*, 6, 1930

It is said . . . you cannot change human nature. On the other hand, it is maintained that human nature is the easiest thing in the world to change if you catch it young enough.
—GEORGE BERNARD SHAW, BBC radio talk, June 18, 1935, in Lawrence, ed., *Platform & Pulpit* (1961)

Man is not the sum of what he has but the totality of what he does not yet have, of what he might have.
—JEAN-PAUL SARTRE, *Situations*, 1, 1939

There is no human nature, since there is no God to conceive it. Not only is man what he conceives himself to be, but he is also only what he wills himself to be.
—JEAN-PAUL SARTRE, *Existentialism is a Humanism*, "The Humanism of Existentialism," 1947

Man is the only animal that can be *bored*, that can feel evicted from paradise. Man is the only animal who finds his own existence a problem which he has to solve and from which he cannot escape.
—ERICH FROMM, *The Sane Society*, III, 1955

The myth of early man's aggressiveness belongs in the same class as the myth of "the beast," that is, the belief that most if not all "wild" animals are ferocious killers. In the same class belongs the myth of "the jungle," "the wild," "the warfare of nature," and, of course, the myth of "innate depravity" or "original sin." These myths represent the projection of our *acquired* human deplorabilities upon the screen of "nature."
—ASHLEY MONTAGU, *Man Observed*, 15, 1968

A vision of a future social order is based on a concept of human nature. If in fact humans are indefinitely malleable, completely plastic beings, with no innate structures of mind and no intrinsic needs of a cultural or social character, then they are fit subjects for the "shaping of behavior" by the state authority, the corporate manager, the technocrat, or the central committee. Those with some confidence in the human species will hope this is not so.
—NOAM CHOMSKY, "Language and Freedom," *Abraxis*, I, 1, 1970

The patterns of human social behavior, including altruistic behavior, are under genetic control, in the sense that they represent a restricted subset of possible patterns that are very different from the patterns of termites, chimpanzees, and other animal species.
—EDWARD O. WILSON, letter in *The New York Times Magazine*, November 30, 1975

Why imagine that specific genes for aggression, dominance, or spite have any importance when we know that the brain's enormous flexibility permits us to be aggressive or peaceful, dominant or submissive, spiteful or generous?
—STEPHEN J. GOULD, *Ever Since Darwin*, "Biological Potentiality vs. Biological Determinism," 1977

The Passions

I have laboured carefully not to mock, lament, or denounce human actions, but to understand them; and to this end I have looked upon

passions such as love, hatred, anger, envy, ambition, pity, and the other perturbations of the mind, not in the light of vices of human nature, but as properties just as pertinent to it as are heat, cold, storm, thunder, and the like to the nature of the atmosphere.
—BENEDICT DE SPINOZA, *Political Treatise*, I, 4, 1677

An emotion becomes more under our control, and the mind is less passive in respect to it, in proportion as it is more known to us.
—BENEDICT DE SPINOZA, *Ethics*, V, 3, "Corollary," 1677

They talked of the passions. "Ah! how fatal are their effects!" said Zadig. "They are the winds that swell the sails of the ship," replied the hermit; "It is true, they sometimes sink her, but without them she could not sail at all. The bile makes us sick and choleric, but without the bile we could not live."
—VOLTAIRE, *Zadig*, 18, 1747

It is by the activity of our passions that our reason is improved; for we desire knowledge only because we desire enjoyment; and it is impossible to conceive any reason why a person who has neither fears nor desires should give himself the trouble of reasoning.
—JEAN-JACQUES ROUSSEAU, *Discourse on the Origin and Foundations of Inequality among Men*, 1755

The passions are neither good nor evil dispositions till they receive a direction. . . . Reason must hold the rudder, or, let the wind blow which way it list, the vessel will never advance smoothly to its destined point.
—MARY WOLLSTONECRAFT, *Vindication of the Rights of Men*, 1790

Prudence is a rich ugly old maid courted by Incapacity. He who desires but acts not, breeds pestilence.
—WILLIAM BLAKE, *The Marriage of Heaven and Hell*, 1793

We reason deeply when we forcibly feel.
—MARY WOLLSTONECRAFT, *Letters Written during a Short Residence in Sweden, Norway, and Denmark*, 1796

Passion, though a bad regulator, is a powerful spring.
—RALPH WALDO EMERSON, *The Conduct of Life*, "Considerations by the Way," 1860

At one time you had wild dogs in your cellar, but they changed over time into birds and lovely singers. Out of your poisons you brewed your balsam.
—FRIEDRICH NIETZSCHE, *Thus Spoke Zarathustra*, I, 5, 1883

The misunderstanding of passion and *reason*: as if the latter existed as an entity by itself, and not rather as a state of the relations between different passions and desires; and as if every passion did not contain in itself its own quantum of reason.
—FRIEDRICH NIETZSCHE, *The Will to Power* (Kaufmann transl.), 387, 1887-88

The church combats passion by excision; its remedy is castration. It never inquires how desire can be spiritualized, beautified, deified.
—FRIEDRICH NIETZSCHE, *The Twilight of the Idols*, "Morality as Anti-Nature," 1, 1889

It is feeling that sets a man thinking, and not thought that sets him feeling.
—GEORGE BERNARD SHAW, "The Religion of the Pianoforte," in *Music in London* (1930), 1894

Every desire has enriched me more than the possession of the always false object of any of them.
—ANDRÉ GIDE, *Fruits of the Earth*, I, 1, 1897

A Rationalist may or may not be emotional, but he knows that emotion has its honoured place in life. . . . He calls himself the champion of reason because in the past reason has been too little consulted, and authority and emotion too much, in the formation of beliefs. Undoubtedly he admits that there are more things in life than reason, because there are more tasks in life than the formation of opinions.
—JOSEPH MCCABE, *The Religion of Woman*, "The Religious Instinct," 1905

We think we can have our emotions for nothing. We cannot. Even the finest and most self-sacrificing emotions have to be paid for. Strangely enough, that is what makes them fine.
—OSCAR WILDE, *De Profundis*, 1905

My great religion is a belief in the blood, the flesh, as being wiser than the intellect. . . . I conceive a man's body as a kind of flame, like a candle flame, forever upright and yet flowing: and the intellect is just the light that is shed on to the things around.
—D. H. LAWRENCE, letter to Ernest Collins, January 13, 1913

Reason is not a force contrary to the passions, but a harmony possible among them. Except in their interests it could have no ardour, except in their world it could have no point of application, nothing to beautify, nothing to dominate.
—GEORGE SANTAYANA, *The Realm of Matter*, VIII, 1930

Much of what is greatest in human achievement involves some element of intoxication, some sweeping away of prudence by passion. Without the Bacchic element, life would be uninteresting; with it, it is dangerous.
—BERTRAND RUSSELL, *History of Western Philosophy*, I, 1, 1, 1945

Pain. Pleasure

When, therefore, we maintain that pleasure is the end, we do not mean the pleasures of profligates and those that consist in sensuality . . . but freedom from pain in the body and from trouble in the mind.
—EPICURUS, *Letter to Menoeceus*, 4th-3rd century B.C.

No pleasure is a bad thing in itself: but the means which produce some pleasures bring with them disturbances many times greater than the pleasures.
—EPICURUS, *Principal Doctrines*, 4th-3rd century B.C.

Assuredly nothing forbids man to enjoy himself, save grim and gloomy superstition. . . . Therefore, to make use of what comes in

our way, and to enjoy it as much as possible (not to the point of satiety, for that would not be enjoyment) is the part of a wise man.
—BENEDICT DE SPINOZA, *Ethics*, IV, 45, "Note," 1677

Nature has placed mankind under the government of two sovereign masters, *pain* and *pleasure*. . . . They govern us in all we do, in all we say, in all we think: every effort we can make to throw off our subjection will serve but to demonstrate and confirm it.
—JEREMY BENTHAM, *An Introduction to the Principles of Morals and Legislation*, 1, 1789

A certain amount of care or pain or trouble is necessary for every man at all times. A ship without ballast is unstable and will not go straight.
—ARTHUR SCHOPENHAUER, *Parerga and Paralipomena*, Vol. II, 12, 1851

It is only great pain, the long slow pain which takes time, by which we are burned as it were with green wood, that compels us philosophers to descend into our ultimate depths and to divest ourselves of all trust, all good-nature. . . . I doubt whether such pain "improves" us; but I know that it *deepens* us.
—FRIEDRICH NIETZSCHE, *The Gay Science* (Kaufmann transl.), "Preface" to the 2nd edition, 1886

Man, the bravest of the animals and the one most inured to suffering, does not repudiate suffering in itself: he wills it, he even seeks it out, provided he can find a meaning in it, a purpose for it.
—FRIEDRICH NIETZSCHE, *The Genealogy of Morals*, 3, 1887

That which does not destroy me, makes me stronger.
—FRIEDRICH NIETZSCHE, *Twilight of the Idols* (Kaufmann transl.), "Maxims and Arrows," 8, 1889

Whatever ascetic morality . . . may say, pleasures and pains are the incentives and restraints by which Nature keeps her progeny from destruction.
—HERBERT SPENCER, *Essays*, "Representative Government," 1891

Pleasure is Nature's test, her sign of approval. When man is happy, he is in harmony with himself and his environment.
—OSCAR WILDE, "The Soul of Man under Socialism," *Fortnightly Review*, February, 1891

Self-denial is simply a method by which man arrests his progress, and self-sacrifice a survival of the mutilation of the savage, part of that old worship of pain which is so terrible a factor in the history of the world.
—OSCAR WILDE, *Intentions*, "The Critic as Artist," 1891

A cigarette is the perfect type of a perfect pleasure. It is exquisite, and it leaves one unsatisfied. What more can one want?
—OSCAR WILDE, *The Picture of Dorian Gray*, 6, 1891

I have drunk many wines since then, but I have known none of them that give the intoxication that comes from fasting.
—ANDRÉ GIDE, *Fruits of the Earth*, IV, 1, 1897

To deny that pleasure is good and pain an evil is a grotesque affectation: it amounts to giving "good" and "evil" artificial definitions and thereby reducing ethics to arbitrary verbiage.
—GEORGE SANTAYANA, *Reason in Common Sense*, 2, 1905

It is often only through a lack of imagination that one does not suffer so much.
—MARCEL PROUST, *Sodom et Gomorrhe*, "Brusque revirement vers Albertine," 1921-22

There are moments in life when a kind of beauty is created from the multiplicity of troubles that assail us, interweaving like Wagnerian leitmotifs.
—MARCEL PROUST, *Albertine disparue*, "Le chagrin et l'oublie," 1925

An objective impression differs according to the interior state in which one approaches it. And pain is as powerful a transformer of reality as drunkenness.
—MARCEL PROUST, *Albertine disparu*, "Le chagrin et l'oublie," 1925

I knew that suffering did not ennoble; it degraded. It made men selfish, mean, petty, and suspicious. It absorbed them in small things. . . . it made them less than men; and I wrote ferociously that we learn resignation not by our own suffering, but by the suffering of others.
—W. SOMERSET MAUGHAM, *The Summing Up*, 19, 1938

The gods had condemned Sisyphus to ceaselessly rolling a rock to the top of a mountain, whence the stone would fall back of its own

weight. They had thought with some reason that there is no more dreadful punishment than futile and hopeless labor. . . . [But] the lucidity that was to constitute his torture at the same time crowns his victory. There is no fate that cannot be surmounted by scorn.
—ALBERT CAMUS, *The Myth of Sisyphus*, "The Myth of Sisyphus," 1942

The Individual

No bird soars too high if he soars with his own wings.
—WILLIAM BLAKE, *Marriage of Heaven and Hell*, 1793

A man's life should be a stately march to a sweet but unheard music, and when to his fellows it shall seem irregular and inharmonious, he will only be stepping to a livelier measure, or his nicer ear hurry him into a thousand symphonies and concordant variations.
—HENRY DAVID THOREAU, *Journal*, June 30, 1840

I – this thought which is called I – is the mould into which the world is poured like melted wax.
—RALPH WALDO EMERSON, "The Transcendentalist," in *Nature; Addresses, and Lectures* (1849), 1842

A man of correct insight among those who are duped and deluded resembles one whose watch is right while all the clocks in the town give the wrong time. He alone knows the correct time, but of what

use is this to him? The whole world is guided by the clocks that show the wrong time.
—ARTHUR SCHOPENHAUER, *Parerga and Paralipomena*, Vol. I, "Aphorisms on the Wisdom of Life," 5, 1851

Precisely because the tyranny of opinion is such as to make eccentricity a reproach, it is desirable, in order to break through that tyranny, that people should be eccentric. Eccentricity has always abounded when and where strength of character has abounded.
—JOHN STUART MILL, *On Liberty*, 5, 1859

We should all remember that to be like other people is to be unlike ourselves, and that nothing can be more detestable in character than servile imitation. . . . The poorest bargain that a human being can make is to give his individuality for what is called respectability.
—ROBERT G. INGERSOLL, *Individuality*, 1873

All history is a record of the power of minorities, and of minorities of one.
—RALPH WALDO EMERSON, *Letters and Social Aims*, "Progress of Culture," 1876

So long as you are praised think only that you are not yet on your own path but on that of another.
—FRIEDRICH NIETZSCHE, *Assorted Opinions and Maxims* (Hollingdale transl.), 340, 1879

Insanity in individuals is something rare – but in groups, parties, nations, and epochs it is the rule.
—FRIEDRICH NIETZSCHE, *Beyond Good and Evil* (Kaufmann transl.), IV, 156, 1886

Great Freethinkers

One of the unpardonable sins, in the eyes of most people, is for a man to go about unlabelled. The world regards such a person as the police do an unmuzzled dog, not under proper control.
—THOMAS HUXLEY, *Collected Essays*, Vol. IX, "Science and Morals," 1886

The recognition of private property has really harmed Individualism, and obscured it, by confusing a man with what he possesses. . . . It has debarred one part of the community from being individual by starving them. It has debarred the other part of the community from being individual by putting them on the wrong road, and encumbering them.
—OSCAR WILDE, "The Soul of Man under Socialism," *Fortnightly Review*, February, 1891

Ah! don't say you agree with me. When people agree with me I always feel that I must be wrong.
—OSCAR WILDE, *Intentions*, "The Critic as Artist," 1891

It is tragic how few people ever "possess their souls" before they die. . . . Most people are other people. Their thoughts are someone else's opinions, their lives a mimicry, their passions a quotation.
—OSCAR WILDE, *De Profundis*, 1905

A biography is considered complete if it merely accounts for six or seven selves, whereas a person may well have as many as a thousand.
—VIRGINIA WOOLF, *Orlando*, 1928

The virtues that are supposed to attend rugged individualism may be vocally proclaimed, but . . . what is cherished is measured by its connection with those activities that make for success in business conducted for personal gain. Hence, the irony of the gospel of "individualism" in business conjoined with suppression of individuality in thought and speech.
—JOHN DEWEY, *Individualism Old and New*. Quoted in Ratner, ed., *Intelligence in the Modern World* (1939), VI, 1, 1930

I am truly a "lone traveler" and have never belonged to my country, my home, my friends, or even my immediate family, with my whole heart. In the face of all these ties, I have never lost a sense of distance and the need for solitude.
—ALBERT EINSTEIN, *Ideas and Opinions* (1954), "The World as I See It," 1930

Every individual is, as it were, a sort of experiment made by nature to test this and that group of qualities.
—H. G. WELLS, statement in Einstein et. al., *Living Philosophies*, 1931

Let each one as an individual assume the roles of artist, healer, prophet, priest, king, warrior, saint. No division of labor. Let us recombine the dispersed elements of our individuality. Let us reintegrate.
—HENRY MILLER, *The Cosmological Eye*, "An Open Letter to Surrealists Everywhere," 1939

The individual is a myth. There are no individuals. . . . It is because a person derives his self and develops it through his interrelationships with other selves that there is not nor can there ever be such a thing as an individual – separate and apart from other selves.
—ASHLEY MONTAGU, *The Humanization of Man*, I, 4, 1962

Love. Friendship

I like a . . . friendship that prides itself on the sharpness and vigor of its intercourse, as love does in bites and scratches that draw blood. It is not vigorous and liberal enough if it is not quarrelsome, if it is tame and artificial, if it fears upsets and walks in constraint.
—MICHEL DE MONTAIGNE, *Essays*, III, 8, 1588

One first knows that one exists when one rediscovers oneself in others.
—JOHANN WOLFGANG VON GOETHE, letter to Auguste Stolberg, February 13, 1775

People are united by sentiments and divided by opinions. . . . The friendships of youth are based on the former, the cliques of old age are the result of the latter. If we could become aware of this . . . we would be more accommodating and would seek to bring together through sentiment what has been scattered by opinion.
—JOHANN WOLFGANG VON GOETHE, letter to F. Jacobi, January 6, 1813

Love, and you shall be loved. All love is mathematically just, as much as the two sides of the algebraic equation.
—RALPH WALDO EMERSON, *Essays*, First Series, "Compensation," 1841

Ignorance and bungling with love are better than wisdom and skill without.
—HENRY DAVID THOREAU, *Journal*, March 25, 1842

We must accept or refuse one another as we are. I could tame a hyena more easily than my Friend. He is a material which no tool of mine will work.
—HENRY DAVID THOREAU, *A Week on the Concord and Merrimack Rivers*, "Wednesday," 1849

We do not love people so much for the good they have done us, as for the good we have done them.
—LEO TOLSTOY, *War and Peace*, I, 16, 1862

Fellowship in joy, not sympathy in sorrow, makes the friend.
—FRIEDRICH NIETZSCHE, *Human All-Too-Human*, 499, 1878

The love of *one* is a barbarism; for it is exercised at the expense of all others. The love of God, too.
—FRIEDRICH NIETZSCHE, *Beyond Good and Evil* (Kaufmann transl.), IV, 67, 1886

Anybody can sympathise with the sufferings of a friend, but it requires a very fine nature – it requires, in fact, the nature of a true Individualist – to sympathise with a friend's success.
—OSCAR WILDE, "The Soul of Man under Socialism," *Fortnightly Review*, February, 1891

My claim was not to love anyone in particular – man or woman – but friendship itself, or affection, or love. I refused to deprive another of what I gave to one, and would only *lend* myself, just as I had no wish to appropriate another's body or heart.
—ANDRÉ GIDE, *Fruits of the Earth*, IV, I, 1897

The world is wonderful and beautiful and good beyond one's wildest imagination. Never, never, never could one conceive what love is, beforehand, never.

—D. H. LAWRENCE, letter to Sallie Hopkin, June 2, 1912. Written shortly after meeting Frieda Weekley, whom he later married

I do not spark automatically, but must have other minds to rub up against, and strike from them by friction the spark that will kindle my thoughts.

—RANDOLPH BOURNE, *Youth and Life*, "The Excitement of Friendship," 1913

Our friends are chosen for us by some hidden law of sympathy, and not by our conscious wills. . . . We get the full quality of their personality at the first shock of meeting, and no future intimacy changes that quality.

—RANDOLPH BOURNE, *Youth and Life*, "The Excitement of Friendship," 1913

We let ourselves out piecemeal it seems, so that only with a host of varied friends can we express ourselves to the fullest. Each friend calls out some particular trait in us, and it requires the whole chorus fitly to teach us what we are.

—RANDOLPH BOURNE, *Youth and Life*, "The Excitement of Friendship," 1913

Instead of defending "free love", which is a much-abused term capable of many interpretations, we ought to strive for the freedom of love; for while the former has come to imply freedom of any sort

of love, the latter must only mean freedom for a feeling which is worthy the name of love.
—ELLEN KEY, *Spreading Liberty and the Great Libertarians*, 1913

Each friend represents a world in us, a world possibly not born until they arrive, and it is only by this meeting that a new world is born.
—ANAÏS NIN, *The Diary of Anaïs Nin*, Vol. II (1967), March, 1937

If an individual is able to love productively, he loves himself too; if he can love *only* others, he cannot love at all.
—ERICH FROMM, *The Art of Loving*, II, 3, 1956

Love, by its very nature, is unworldly, and it is for this reason rather than its rarity that it is not only apolitical but antipolitical, perhaps the most powerful of all antipolitical human forces.
—HANNAH ARENDT, *The Human Condition*, V, 33, 1958

Love is the perception of individuals. Love is the extremely difficult realisation that something other than oneself is real. Love, and so art and morals, is the discovery of reality.
—IRIS MURDOCH, *Existentialists and Mystics* (1997), "The Sublime and the Good," 1959

Habit. Convention

Custom is truly a violent and deceitful schoolmistress. She establishes in us, little by little, furtively, a foothold for her authority; but

having, by this mild and humble beginning, fixed and planted it with the aid of time, she soon discloses to us a furious and tyrannical face against which we no longer have the liberty of even raising our eyes.
—MICHEL DE MONTAIGNE, *Essays*, I, 23, 1580

A long habit of not thinking a thing wrong gives it a superficial appearance of being right and raises at first a formidable outcry in defense of custom.
—THOMAS PAINE, *Common Sense*, "Introduction," 1776

Man's good intentions, resolutions that inevitably succumb to ingrained habit, are like the cleaning, scrubbing, and adorning that we practice on Sundays, holidays, and feast days. We always get dirty again, to be sure, but such a partial cleaning process has the advantage of upholding the principle of cleanliness.
—JOHANN WOLFGANG VON GOETHE, conversations with Riemer (Weigand transl.), November, 1806

We do everything by custom, even believe by it; our very axioms, let us boast of freethinking as we may, are oftenest simply such beliefs as we have never heard questioned.
—THOMAS CARLYLE, *Sartor Resartus*, 3, 1836

Without the aid of prejudice and custom, I should not be able to find my way across the room.
—WILLIAM HAZLITT, "On Prejudice," in *Sketches and Essays*, 1839

The interrogation of custom at all points is an inevitable stage in the growth of every superior mind.

—RALPH WALDO EMERSON, *Representative Men*, "Montaigne," 1850

The tradition of the dead generations weighs like a nightmare on the brain of the living. And just when they seem engaged in revolutionising themselves and things in creating something entirely new, precisely in such epochs of revolutionary crisis they anxiously conjure up the spirits of the past to their service.

—KARL MARX, *The Eighteenth Brumaire of Louis Bonaparte*, 1, 1852

The tyrant, Custom, has been summoned before the bar of Common-Sense. His majesty no longer awes the multitude – his scepter is broken – his crown is trampled in the dust – the sentence of death is pronounced upon him.

—ELIZABETH CADY STANTON, speech to N.Y. State Legislature, February 14, 1854. Quoted in Stanton et. al., *History of Woman Suffrage*, Vol. I

It is remarkable how easily and insensibly we fall into a particular route, and make a beaten track for ourselves. I had not lived there a week before my feet wore a path from my door to the pond-side; and though it is five or six years since I trod it, it is still quite distinct.

—HENRY DAVID THOREAU, *Walden*, "Conclusion," 1854

The favorite phrase of English law is, "a custom whereof the memory of man runneth not back to the contrary."

—RALPH WALDO EMERSON, *English Traits*, "Manners," 1856

Custom meets us at the cradle and leaves us only at the tomb. Our first questions are answered by ignorance, and our last by superstition.
—ROBERT G. INGERSOLL, *Individuality*, 1873

Habit is the enormous fly-wheel of society, its most precious conservative agent.
—WILLIAM JAMES, *The Principles of Psychology*, 4, 1890

Could the young but realize how soon they will become mere walking bundles of habits, they would give more heed to their conduct while in the plastic state.
—WILLIAM JAMES, *The Principles of Psychology*, 4, 1890

Customs embody the rule of the dead over the living; as do also the laws into which they harden.
—HERBERT SPENCER, *The Principles of Ethics*, 121, 1892

Habit is habit, and not to be flung out of the window by any man, but coaxed down-stairs a step at a time.
—MARK TWAIN, *The Tragedy of Pudd'nhead Wilson*, 6, "Pudd'nhead Wilson's Calendar," 1894

One may no more live in the world without picking up the moral prejudices of the world than one will be able to go to hell without perspiring.
—H.L. MENCKEN, *Prejudices*, Second Series, V, 1920

Rigid, the skeleton of habit alone upholds the human frame.
—VIRGINIA WOOLF, *Mrs. Dalloway*, 1925

We only truly know what is new, that which strikes our senses through an abrupt change and for which habit has not yet substituted its pale facsimiles.
—MARCEL PROUST, *Albertine disparue*, "Le chagrin et l'oublie," 1925

The reason why sensible people are as conventional as they can bear to be is that conventionality saves so much time and thought and trouble and social friction of one sort or another that it leaves them much more leisure for freedom than unconventionality does.
—GEORGE BERNARD SHAW, *The Intelligent Woman's Guide to Socialism and Capitalism*, 79, 1928

Conventional people are roused to fury by departure from convention, largely because they regard such departure as a criticism of themselves.
—BERTRAND RUSSELL, *The Conquest of Happiness*, 9, 1930

While other animals are mostly creatures of habitat, man is the creature of habit – habits which he acquires from his culture.
—ASHLEY MONTAGU, *The Humanization of Man*, I, 1, 1962

Clichés, stock phrases, adherence to conventional, standardized codes of expression and conduct have the socially recognized function of protecting us against reality, that is, against the claim on our thinking attention that all events and facts make by virtue of their existence.
—HANNAH ARENDT, *The Life of the Mind*, Vol. I, "Introduction," 1978

"Roles," after all, are not fit aspirations for adults, but the repetitive performances of people who have forgotten that it is only other people who write the scripts.
—BARBARA EHRENREICH, *The Hearts of Men*, 11, 1983

Education

Only one who bursts with eagerness do I instruct; only one who bubbles with excitement do I enlighten. If I hold up one corner and a man cannot come back to me with the other three, I do not continue the lesson.
—CONFUCIUS, *Analects* (Waley transl.), VII, 8, 6th-5th century B.C.

One should inquire not who is the most learned but who is the best learned.
—MICHEL DE MONTAIGNE, *Essays*, I, 25, 1580

Tim was so learned, that he could name a Horse in nine Languages; So ignorant, that he bought a Cow to ride on.
—BENJAMIN FRANKLIN, *Poor Richard's Almanack*, 1750

The first education should be purely negative. It consists not in teaching virtue or truth, but in guarding the heart from vice and the mind from error.
—JEAN-JACQUES ROUSSEAU, *Émile ou de l'éducation*, II, 1762

Our first masters of philosophy are our feet, our hands, our eyes. To substitute books for these things is not to teach us to reason, it is to teach us to avail ourselves of the reason of others; it is to teach us to believe much and to never know anything.
—JEAN-JACQUES ROUSSEAU, *Émile ou de l'éducation*, II, 1762

Men and women must be educated, in a great degree, by the opinions and manners of the society they live in. . . . It may then fairly be inferred, that, till society be differently constituted, much cannot be expected from education.
—MARY WOLLSTONECRAFT, *A Vindication of the Rights of Woman*, 1792

Every good book, especially those of the ancients, can be understood and enjoyed only by him who has something of his own to contribute. He who knows something finds infinitely more in them than he who comes merely to learn.
—JOHANN WOLFGANG VON GOETHE, *On Theory of Color* (Weigand transl.), 1810

What does education often do? It makes a straight-cut ditch of a free, meandering brook.
—HENRY DAVID THOREAU, *Journal*, October 31, 1850

There is no absurdity so palpable but that it may be firmly planted in the human head if you only begin to inculcate it before the age of five, by constantly repeating it with an air of great solemnity. For as in the case of animals, . . . training is successful only when you begin in early youth.
—ARTHUR SCHOPENHAUER, *Parerga and Paralipomena*, Vol. II, 26, 1851

We seem to have forgotten that the expression "a *liberal* education" originally meant among the Romans one worthy of *free* men; while the learning of trades and professions by which to get your livelihood merely was considered worthy of *slaves* only.
—HENRY DAVID THOREAU, "The Last Days of John Brown," in *A Yankee in Canada, with Anti-Slavery and Reform Papers* (1866), 1860

The education of the future will in the case of every child over a certain age combine productive labor with education and athletics not merely as one of the methods of raising social production but as the only method of producing fully developed human beings.
—KARL MARX, *Capital*, Vol. I, 13, 9, 1867

It is because the body is a machine that education is possible. Education is the formation of habits, a superinducing of an artificial organisation upon the natural organisation of the body; so that acts, which at first required a conscious effort, eventually became unconscious and mechanical.
—THOMAS H. HUXLEY, *Collected Essays*, Vol. I, "On Descartes' 'Discourse on Method'," 1870

I am firmly persuaded that every unnatural activity of the brain is as mischievous as any unnatural activity of the body, and that pressing people to learn things they do not want to know is as unwholesome and disastrous as feeding them on sawdust.
—GEORGE BERNARD SHAW, *Immaturity* (1930), 1879

The whole art of teaching is only the art of awakening the natural curiosity of young minds for the purpose of satisfying it afterwards.
—ANATOLE FRANCE, *The Crime of Silvestre Bonnard*, II, 4, 1881

One repays a teacher badly if one always remains merely a student. And why do you not want to pluck at my wreath?
—FRIEDRICH NIETZSCHE, *Thus Spoke Zarathustra*, I, 22, 1883

Education is an admirable thing, but it is well to remember from time to time that nothing that is worth knowing can be taught.
—OSCAR WILDE, *Intentions*, "The Critic as Artist," 1891

In the first place God made idiots. This was for practice. Then He made School Boards.
—MARK TWAIN, *Following the Equator*, Vol. II, 25, "Pudd'nhead Wilson's New Calendar," 1897

Our methods of education have been especially esteemed, not because they taught the child to like what he did, but taught him to do what he did not like. We take it for granted that he will not like his life work, and so seek to fit him for continued application to distasteful service.
—CHARLOTTE PERKINS GILMAN, *Human Work*, 16, 1904

Education: That which discloses to the wise and disguises from the foolish their lack of understanding.
—AMBROSE BIERCE, *The Devil's Dictionary*, 1906

At every step the child should be allowed to meet the real experiences of life; the thorns should never be plucked from his roses.
—ELLEN KEY, *The Century of the Child*, 3, 1909

It is noble to teach oneself; it is still nobler to teach others – and less trouble.
—MARK TWAIN, *Mark Twain's Speeches*, "Introducing Doctor Van Dyke," 1910

The child is a natural born "rubber neck." His curiosity is alert. Give him the chance and he will learn. One glance, if he sees the thing himself, is better than two hours of studying about a thing which he does not see.
—THOMAS A. EDISON, *The Diary and Sundry Observations* (1948), 1914

And this is the way to educate children: the instinctive way of mothers. There should be no effort made to teach children to think, to have ideas. Only to lift them and urge them into dynamic activity.

—D. H. LAWRENCE, *Fantasia of the Unconscious*, 1922

Interest and simplicity should be the keynotes of all education, I believe. It is impossible to fascinate young minds with dull complexities.

—THOMAS A. EDISON, *The Diary and Sundry Observations* (1948), 1927

The sentiments of an adult are compounded of a kernal of instinct surrounded by a vast husk of education.

—BERTRAND RUSSELL, *Sceptical Essays*, 15, 1928

Hardly any [of our children] are introduced to the scientific outlook until their minds have been so filled with pre-scientific ideas as to make scientific thought very difficult.

—J. B. S. HALDANE, *The Inequality of Man and Other Essays*, "What I Think About," 1932

There is no subject that is in and of itself, or without regard to the stage of growth attained by the learner, such that inherent educational value can be attributed to it. . . . There is no such thing as educational value in the abstract.

—JOHN DEWEY, *Experience and Education*, 3, 1938

The notion that every problem can be studied as such with an open and empty mind, without preconception, without knowing what

has already been learned about it, must condemn men to a chronic childishness. For no man, and no generation of men, is capable of inventing for itself the arts and sciences of a high civilization.
—WALTER LIPPMANN, "Education vs. Western Civilization," *The American Scholar*, 10, 1941. Quoted in Rossiter & Lare, eds., *The Essential Lippmann* (1963)

In the educational system of a democracy, the authority of method must ultimately replace the authority of persons and institutions in the determination of truth.
—SIDNEY HOOK, *Education for Modern Man*, 6, 1946

The teacher's qualification consists in knowing the world and being able to instruct others about it, but his authority rests on his assumption of responsibility for that world.
—HANNAH ARENDT, *Between Past and Future*, "The Crisis in Education," 1961

Maybe the chief mistake we make is to pay too much *direct* attention to the "education" of children and adolescents, rather than providing them a worthwhile adult world in which to grow up. In a curious way, the exaggeration of schooling is both a harsh exploitation of the young, regimenting them for the social machine, and a compassionate coddling of them.
—PAUL GOODMAN, *Compulsory Mis-Education*, II, 11, 1964

Liberating education consists in acts of cognition, not transferrals of information.
—PAULO FREIRE, *Pedagogy of the Oppressed*, 2, 1970

Education must begin with the solution of the teacher-student contradiction, by reconciling the poles of the contradiction so that both are simultaneously teachers *and* students.
—PAULO FREIRE, *Pedagogy of the Oppressed*, 2, 1970

Humor. Irony

In laughter there is always a kind of joyousness that is incompatible with contempt or indignation.
—VOLTAIRE, *L'Enfant prodigue*, "Preface," 1736

Woe to philosophers who cannot laugh away their learned wrinkles! I look on solemnity as a disease. . . . It seems to me that morality, study, and gaiety are three sisters who should never be separated: they are your servants; I take them as my mistresses.
—VOLTAIRE, letter to Frederick the Great, July, 1737

Wit and humor, like all corrosives, must be used with care.
—GEORG CHRISTOF LICHTENBERG, *Aphorisms*, in Mautner & Hatfield, eds., *The Lichtenberg Reader* (1959), 1768-71

The man of Humour sees common life, even mean life, under the new light of sportfulness and love; whatever has existence has a charm for him. Humour has justly been regarded as the finest perfection of poetic genius.
—THOMAS CARLYLE, *Critical and Miscellaneous Essays*, "Schiller," 1838

Laughter and tears are meant to turn the wheels of the same sensibility; one is wind-power, the other is water-power, that is all.
—OLIVER WENDELL HOLMES, *The Autocrat of the Breakfast-Table*, 4, 1858

Socrates excels the founder of Christianity in being able to be serious cheerfully and in possessing that *wisdom full of roguishness* that constitutes the finest state of the human soul.
—FRIEDRICH NIETZSCHE, *The Wanderer and his Shadow* (Hollingdale transl.), 86, 1878

Humor sees both sides. While reason is the holy light, humor carries the lantern, and the man with a keen sense of humor is preserved from the solemn stupidities of superstition.
—ROBERT G. INGERSOLL, *What Must be Done to be Saved*, 1880

Life is far too important a thing ever to talk seriously about.
—OSCAR WILDE, *Lady Windermere's Fan*, III, 1892

To laugh without sympathy is a ruinous abuse of a noble function.
—GEORGE BERNARD SHAW, "The Farcical Comedy Outbreak," in *Our Theatres in the Nineties* (1930), 1896

A sense of humour keen enough to show a man his own absurdities, as well as those of other people, will keep him from the commission of all sins, or nearly all save those that are worth committing.
—SAMUEL BUTLER, *Notebooks*, "Lord, What is Man?" (1912), late 19th century

No matter how much restriction civilization imposes on the individual, he nevertheless finds some way to circumvent it. Wit is the best safety valve modern man has evolved; the more civilization, the more repression, the more need there is for wit.

—SIGMUND FREUD, *Wit and its Relation to the Unconscious*, 1905

This Christian Church . . . is giving way to that older and greater Church [the theatre] to which I belong: the Church where the oftener you laugh the better, because by laughter only can you destroy evil without malice, and affirm good fellowship without mawkishness.

—GEORGE BERNARD SHAW, "The Author's Apology," in *Our Theatres in the Nineties* (1930), 1906

Irony was Greek, with all the free, happy play of the Greek spirit about it, letting in fresh air and light into others' minds and our own. It was to the Greek an incomparable method of intercourse, the rub of mind against mind by the simple use of simulated ignorance and the adoption, without committing one's self, of another's point of view.

—RANDOLPH BOURNE, *Youth and Life*, "The Life of Irony," 1913

The ironist is the great intellectual democrat, in whose presence and before whose law all ideas and attitudes stand equal. In his world there is no privileged caste, no aristocracy of sentiments to be reverenced, or segregated systems of interests to be tabooed. Nothing human is alien to the ironist.

—RANDOLPH BOURNE, *Youth and Life*, "The Life of Irony," 1913

The liberation of the human mind has never been furthered by . . . learned dunderheads; it has been best furthered by gay fellows who heaved dead cats into sanctuaries and then went roistering down the highways of the world, proving to all men that doubt, after all, was safe – that the god in the sanctuary was finite in his power, and hence a fraud. One horse-laugh is worth 10,000 syllogisms.
—H. L. MENCKEN, *Prejudices*, Fourth Series, VII, 2, 1924

Humor is not resigned; it is rebellious. It signifies not only the triumph of the ego but also of the pleasure principle, which is able to assert itself against the unkindness of the real circumstances.
—SIGMUND FREUD, "Humour," in *Almanach 1928*, 1927

My sense of humor will always stand in the way of seeing myself, my family, my race, or my nation as the whole intent of the universe. When I see what we really are like, I know God is too great an artist for we folks on my side of the creek to be all of His best works.
—ZORA NEALE HURSTON, *Dust Tracks on a Road*, 16, 1942

Humour is not a mood but a way of looking at the world. So if it is correct to say that humour was stamped out in Nazi Germany, that does not mean that people were not in good spirits, or anything of that sort, but something much deeper and more important.
—LUDWIG WITTGENSTEIN, *Culture and Values* (1980), journal entry, 1948

There's a hell of a distance between wisecracking and wit. Wit has truth in it; wisecracking is simply calisthenics with words.
—DOROTHY PARKER, interview in Cowley, ed., *Writer at Work*, 1958

They say the seeds of what we will do are in all of us, but it always seemed to me that in those who make jokes in life the seeds are covered with better soil and with a higher grade of manure.
—ERNEST HEMINGWAY, *A Moveable Feast*, 11, 1964

Sex

In the case of bodily pleasures, is it not unjust to chill the soul regarding them and say that she should be dragged to them as if to some enforced and servile obligation and necessity?
—MICHEL DE MONTAIGNE, *Essays*, III, 5, 1588

I like the Spanish and Italian methods of love-making, more respectful and tentative, more mannered and discrete. I don't know who it was among the ancients who wished for a throat as long as a crane's neck so as to relish longer what he was gulping down.
—MICHEL DE MONTAIGNE, *Essays*, III, 5, 1588

It is a relationship that needs reciprocity and exchange. . . . Indeed in this pastime the pleasure I give tickles my imagination more agreeably than that which I feel.
—MICHEL DE MONTAIGNE, *Essays*, III, 5, 1588

Bury yourself, if you wish, in the dark forest with the perverse companion of your pleasures, but allow the good and simple

Tahitians to reproduce without shame in the sight of heaven in broad daylight.
—DENIS DIDEROT, *Supplement to the Voyage of Bougainville: On the Inconvenience of Attaching Ethical Concepts to Certain Physical Actions to which They are not Appropriate* (1796), 1772

Let . . . no[t] pale religious letchery call that virginity that wishes but acts not!
—WILLIAM BLAKE, *The Marriage of Heaven and Hell*, 1793

It is a piquant element and jest of the world, that the principal concern of all men is pursued secretly and ostensibly ignored as much as possible.
—ARTHUR SCHOPENHAUER, *The World as Will and Idea*, Supplement to Book IV, 42, 1844

The unique and supreme pleasure in love-making lies in the certain knowledge that one is doing *evil*. Men and women know from birth that in evil lies all pleasure of the sense.
—CHARLES BAUDELAIRE, *Journaux intimes*, "Fusées," 71, mid-19th century

Copulation is the lyricism of the masses.
—CHARLES BAUDELAIRE, *Journaux intimes*, "Fusées," 71, mid-19th century

Celibacy is not natural to men or to women; all bodily needs require their legitimate satisfaction, and celibacy is a disregard of natural law.
—ANNIE BESANT, *The Law of Population*, 3, 1878

Christianity gave Eros poison to drink: he did not die of it but degenerated – into a vice.
—FRIEDRICH NIETZSCHE, *Beyond Good and Evil* (Kaufmann transl.), 168, 1886

The preaching of chastity is a public incitement to anti-nature. Every depreciation of sexual life, every sullying of it with the concept "impure," is the ultimate crime against life – is the true sin against the holy spirit of life.
—FRIEDRICH NIETZSCHE, *Ecce Homo* (1908), "Why I Write Such Good Books," 5, 1888

Religion has done love a great service by making it a sin.
—ANATOLE FRANCE, *Le Jardin d'Épicure*, 1894

There can be no sexual love without lust; but, on the other hand, until the currents of lust in the organism have been irradiated as to effect other parts of the psychic organism – at the least the affections and the social feelings – it is not yet sexual love.
—HAVELOCK ELLIS, *Studies in the Psychology of Sex* (1897-1928), "The Valuation of Sexual Love," 1910

Free love? as if love is anything but free. Man has bought brains, but all the millions in the world have failed to buy love.
—EMMA GOLDMAN, *Anarchism and Other Essays*, "Marriage and Love," 1910

We have two tyrannous physical passions: concupiscence and chastity. We become mad in the pursuit of sex; we become equally

mad in the persecution of that pursuit. Unless we gratify our desire the race is lost; unless we restrain it we destroy ourselves.
—GEORGE BERNARD SHAW, *Androcles and the Lion*, "Preface," 1912

A mutual and satisfied sexual act is of great benefit to the average woman; the magnetism of it is health giving. When it is not desired on the part of the woman and she gives no response, it should not take place. The submission of her body without love or desire is degrading to the woman's finer sensibility, all the marriage certificates on earth to the contrary notwithstanding.
—MARGARET SANGER, *Family Limitations*, "Coitus Interruptus," 1914

Sex is, after all, a relatively unimportant and unsatisfying thing in the life of a man. . . . Much more fun is to be got out of the pursuit of knowledge, the furtherance of ambition, the battle for security and dignity.
—H. L. MENCKEN, "Frank Harris Again," *American Mercury*, October, 1925

Life without sex might be safer but it would be unbearably dull. . . . Throttle it, denaturalize it, take it away, and human existence would be reduced to the prosaic, laborious, boresome, imbecile level of life in an anthill.
—H. L. MENCKEN, *New York World*, September 12, 1926

Necessary, forever necessary, [it is] to burn out false shames and smelt the heaviest ore of the body into purity.
—D. H. LAWRENCE, *Lady Chatterley's Lover*, 1928

You mustn't think I advocate perpetual sex. Far from it. Nothing nauseates me more than promiscuous sex in and out of season.
—D. H. LAWRENCE, letter to Lady Ottoline Morrell, December 22, 1928, referring to *Lady Chatterley's Lover*

Regarding sex education: no secrets.
—ALBERT EINSTEIN, letter to the World League for Sexual Reform, Sept. 6, 1929. Quoted in Calaprice, *The Quotable Einstein* (1996)

Morality in sexual relations, when it is free from superstition, consists essentially of respect for the other person, and unwillingness to use that person solely as a means of personal gratification.
—BERTRAND RUSSELL, *Marriage and Morals*, 11, 1929

Civilization is a process in the service of Eros, whose purpose is to combine single human individuals, and after that families, then races, peoples and nations, into one great unity, the unity of mankind.
—SIGMUND FREUD, *Civilization and its Discontents*, 6, 1930

I am against asceticism myself. I am with the old Scotsman who wanted less chastity and more delicacy.
—E. M. FORSTER, *Two Cheers for Democracy* (1951), "What I Believe," 1939

For most women – and men too – it is not a mere matter of satisfying erotic desire, but of maintaining their dignity as human beings while obtaining satisfaction.
—SIMONE DE BEAUVOIR, *The Second Sex*, 25, 1949

In every association an endless debate goes on concerning the ambiguous meaning of the words *give* and *take*: she complains of giving her all, he protests that she takes his all. Woman has to learn that exchanges – it is a fundamental law of political economy – are based on the value the merchandise offered has for the buyer, and not for the seller.
—SIMONE DE BEAUVOIR, *The Second Sex*, "Conclusion," 1949

You mustn't force sex to do the work of love or love to do the work of sex.
—MARY McCARTHY, *The Group*, 2, 1954

Happiness

One enjoys without worry only that which one is able to lose without pain; and if true happiness belongs to the sage, it is because he is of all humans the one from whom fortune can take away the least.
—JEAN-JACQUES ROUSSEAU, *Julie ou la nouvelle Héloïse*, V, 2, 1761

Human felicity is produc'd not so much by great pieces of good fortune that seldom happen, as by little advantages that occur every day. Thus, if you teach a poor young man to shave himself, and keep his razor in order, you may contribute more to the happiness of his life than in giving him a thousand guineas.
—BENJAMIN FRANKLIN, *Autobiography*, 1792

The love of life is, in general, the effect not of our enjoyments, but of our passions.
—WILLIAM HAZLITT, *The Round Table*, "On the Love of Life," 1817

I am too easily contented with a slight and almost animal happiness. My happiness is a good deal like that of the woodchucks.
—HENRY DAVID THOREAU, letter to Harrison Blake, May 2, 1848

To be self-sufficient, to be all in all to oneself, to want for nothing, to be able to say *omnia mea mecum porto* [I carry everything with me] – that is assuredly the chief qualification for happiness.
—ARTHUR SCHOPENHAUER, *Parerga and Paralipomena*, Vol. I, "Aphorisms on the Wisdom of Life," 5, 1851

The two foes of human happiness are pain and boredom. . . . In the degree in which we are fortunate enough to get away from the one, we approach the other. Life presents, in fact, a more or less violent oscillation between the two.
—ARTHUR SCHOPENHAUER, *Parerga and Paralipomena*, Vol. I, "Aphorisms on the Wisdom of Life," 2, 1851

Happiness is not a reward – it is a consequence. Suffering is not a punishment – it is a result.
—ROBERT G. INGERSOLL, *The Christian Religion*, 1881

Precisely the least, the softest, lightest, a lizard's rustling, a breath, a breeze, a moment's glance – it is *little* that makes the *best* happiness.
—FRIEDRICH NIETZSCHE, *Thus Spoke Zarathustra* (Kaufmann transl.), IV, 10, 1885

Take trouble, and turn your trouble into pleasure: that, I shall always hold, is the key to a happy life.
—WILLIAM MORRIS, "The Society of the Future," lecture delivered November 13, 1887

Do not think that my happiness has been made with the help of riches; my heart, freed from all earthly ties, has always been poor, and I shall die easily. My happiness is made of fervour.
—ANDRÉ GIDE, *Fruits of the Earth*, IV, I, 1897

Haven't you noticed that people always exaggerate the value of the things they haven't got? The poor think they need nothing but riches to be quite happy and good. Everybody worships truth, purity, unselfishness, for the same reason: because they have no experience of them.
—GEORGE BERNARD SHAW, Strange Lady in *The Man of Destiny*, 1898

We have no more right to consume happiness without producing it than to consume wealth without producing it.
—GEORGE BERNARD SHAW, *Candida*, I, 1898

He who desires a lifetime of happiness with a beautiful woman desires to enjoy the taste of wine by keeping his mouth always full of it.
—GEORGE BERNARD SHAW, *Man and Superman*, "Maxims for Revolutionists," 1903

To possess it [happiness] means to approach life with the humility of a beggar, but to treat it with the proud generosity of a prince; to bring to its totality the deep understanding of a great poet and to each of its moments the abandonment and ingenuousness of a child.
—ELLEN KEY, *The Morality of Women*, "The Morality of Women," 1911

The secret of being miserable is to have leisure to bother about whether you are happy or not. . . . A perpetual holiday is a good working definition of hell.
—GEORGE BERNARD SHAW, *Misalliance*, "Preface," 1914

Happiness, like health, is probably also only a passing accident. For a moment or two the organism is irritated so little that it is not conscious of it; for the duration of that moment it is happy.
—H. L. MENCKEN, "Comfort for the Ailing," *American Mercury*, March, 1930. Reprinted in *A Mencken Chrestomathy* (1949)

Happiness in the truth is like happiness in marriage: fruitful, lasting, and ironical.
—GEORGE SANTAYANA, *The Realm of Truth*, 14,1937

Work is the nearest thing to happiness that I can find. . . . What all my work shall be, I don't know that either, every hour being a stranger to you until you live it. I want a busy life, a just mind, and a timely death.
—ZORA NEALE HURSTON, *Dust Tracks on a Road*, 16, 1942

A string of excited, fugitive, miscellaneous pleasures is not happiness; happiness resides in imaginative reflection and judgment, when the *picture* of one's life, or of human life, as it truly has been or is, satisfies the will, and is gladly accepted.
—GEORGE SANTAYANA, *The Middle Span*, 1945

Happiness is the criterion of excellence in the art of living, of virtue in the meaning it has in humanistic ethics.
—ERICH FROMM, *Man for Himself*, IV, 3, 1947

Happiness . . . is more than a state of mind. In fact, happiness and unhappiness are expressions of the state of the entire organism, of the total personality. Happiness is conjunctive with an increase in vitality, intensity of feeling and thinking, and productiveness.
—ERICH FROMM, *Man for Himself,* IV, 3, 1947

We can tell whether we are happy by the sound of the wind. It warns the unhappy man of the fragility of his house, hounding him from shallow sleep and violent dreams. To the happy man it is the song of his protectedness: its furious howling concedes that it has power over him no longer.
—THEODOR ADORNO, *Minima Moralia,* 29, 1951

It is not so much the pursuit of happiness as the happiness of pursuit that is most likely to yield gratification, and then only occasionally. . . . Happiness is a by-product, principally of work, and if it is work that one delights in, so much the better.
—ASHLEY MONTAGU, *Man Observed,* 11, 1968

Life

Life is not given for a lasting possession, but merely for use.
—LUCRETIUS, *On the Nature of Things,* III, ca. 50 B.C.

I "pass the time" when it is unpleasant and disagreeable; when it is good, I do not want to pass it; I savor it, I hold it tight.
—MICHEL DE MONTAIGNE, *Essays,* III, 13, 1588

Were it offered to my choice, I should have no objection to a repetition of the same life from its beginning, only asking the advantages authors have in a second edition to correct some faults of the first.
—BENJAMIN FRANKLIN, *Autobiography*, 1791

In closely examining my own and others' course in life and art, I often found that what can properly be called a deviation turned out to be an essential detour for the individual on the way to his ultimate goal. . . . In fact, one often consciously strives for an apparently mistaken goal, just as the ferryman works upstream against the current when his only object is to land just across from his starting point.
—JOHANN WOLFGANG VON GOETHE, letter to Eichstadt, September 15, 1804

Life is a festival only to the wise. Seen from the nook and chimney-side of prudence, it wears a ragged and dangerous front.
—RALPH WALDO EMERSON, *Essays*, First Series, "Heroism," 1841

Life. If any of us knew what we were doing, or whither we were going! We are all dying of miscellany.
—RALPH WALDO EMERSON, *Journals*, May-June, 1843

Each day is a little life: every waking and rising a little birth, every fresh morning a little youth, every going to rest and sleep a little death.
—ARTHUR SCHOPENHAUER, *Parerga and Paralipomena*, Vol. I, "Aphorisms on the Wisdom of Life," 5, 1851

I wanted to live deep and suck out all the marrow of life . . . to drive life into a corner, and reduce it to its lowest terms, and, if it proved

to be mean, why then to get the whole and genuine meanness of it, and publish its meanness to the world; or if it were sublime, to know it by experience, and be able to give a true account of it in my next excursion.
— HENRY DAVID THOREAU, *Walden*, "Where I lived, and what I lived for," 1854

This life is a hospital where each patient desires to change his bed. Over here one would like to suffer in front of the stove, while over there one believes he would be cured next to the window.
—CHARLES BAUDELAIRE, *Le Spleen de Paris*, 48, 1869

If we had keen vision of all that is ordinary in human life, it would be like hearing the grass grow or the squirrel's heart beat, and we should die of the roar which is the other side of silence.
— GEORGE ELIOT, *Middlemarch*, 22, 1871-72

Not the fruit of experience, but experience itself, is the end. A counted number of pulses only is given to us of a variegated, dramatic life. How shall we pass most swiftly from point to point, and be present always at the focus where the greatest number of vital forces unite in their purest energy? To burn always with this hard, gemlike flame, to maintain this ecstasy, is success in life.
—WALTER PATER, *Studies in the History of the Renaissance*, "Conclusion," 1873

The secret of realising the largest productivity and the greatest enjoyment of existence is to live dangerously! Build your cities on the slope of Vesuvius! Send your ships into unexplored seas. Live in war with your equals and with yourselves! Be robbers and

despoilers, you seekers of knowledge, as long as you cannot be rulers and possessors. The time will soon pass when you can be satisfied to live like timid deer concealed in the forests. Knowledge will finally stretch out her hand for that which belongs to her: she means to *rule* and *possess*, and you with it!
—FRIEDRICH NIETZSCHE, *The Gay Science* 283, 1882

This world is a great orange tree filled with blossoms, with ripening and ripened fruit, while, underneath the bending boughs, the fallen slowly turn to dust. Each orange is a life. Let us squeeze it dry, get all the juice there is, so that when death comes we can say: "There is nothing left but withered peel."
—ROBERT G. INGERSOLL, *Which Way?* 10, 1884

And as for the wishes of noble souls: They desire to have nothing for free, least of all life. . . . One should not wish to enjoy where one does not contribute to the enjoyment. And one should not *wish* to enjoy! For enjoyment and innocence are the most bashful things. Neither like to be sought after.
—FRIEDRICH NIETZSCHE, *Thus Spoke Zarathustra*, III, 12, 5, 1884

He who has a *why* for living can bear with almost any *how*.
—FRIEDRICH NIETZSCHE, *Twilight of the Idols*, "Maxims and Missiles," 12, 1889

Life is the art of drawing sufficient conclusions from insufficient premises.
—SAMUEL BUTLER, *Note-Books* (1912), 1, late 19th century

This is the true joy of life, the being used for a purpose recognized by yourself as a mighty one; the being thoroughly worn out before you are thrown on the scrap heap; the being a force of Nature instead of a feverish selfish little clod of ailments and grievances complaining that the world will not devote itself to making you happy.
—GEORGE BERNARD SHAW, *Man and Superman*, "Epistle Dedicatory," 1903

The love of life is not something rational, or founded on experience of life. It is something antecedent and spontaneous.
—GEORGE SANTAYANA, *Three Philosophical Poets*, 2, 1910

To perceive universal mutation, to feel the vanity of life, has always been the beginning of seriousness. It is the condition for any beautiful, measured, or tender philosophy.
—GEORGE SANTAYANA, *Three Philosophical Poets*, 2, 1910

Life is not a campaign of battle, but a laboratory where its possibilities for the enhancement of happiness and the realization of ideals are to be tested and observed. We are not to start life with a code of its laws in our pocket, with its principles of activity already learned by heart, but we are to discover those principles as we go, by conscientious experiment.
—RANDOLPH BOURNE, *Youth and Life*, "The Experimental Life," 1913

Welcome, O life! I go to encounter for the millionth time the reality of experience and to forge in the smithy of my soul the uncreated conscience of my race.
—JAMES JOYCE, *A Portrait of the Artist as a Young Man*, closing words, 1916

There is not one big cosmic meaning for all, there is only the meaning we each give to our life. . . . To seek a total unity is wrong. To give as much meaning to one's life as possible is right to me.
—ANAÏS NIN, *The Diary of Anaïs Nin*, Vol. II (1967), June, 1935

If there is a sin against life, it consists perhaps not so much in despairing of life as in hoping for another life and in eluding the implacable grandeur of this life.
—ALBERT CAMUS, *Summer in Algiers*, 1938

The aim of life is to live, and to live means to be aware, joyously, drunkenly, serenely, divinely, aware.
—HENRY MILLER, *The Wisdom of the Heart*, "Creative Death," 1941

To two men living the same number of years, the world always provides the same sum of experiences. It is up to us to be conscious of them. Being aware of one's life, one's revolt, one's freedom, and to the maximum, is living, and to the maximum.
—ALBERT CAMUS, *The Myth of Sisyphus*, "An Absurd Reasoning," 1942

To say that existence is ambiguous is to assert that its meaning is never fixed, that it must be constantly won.
—SIMONE DE BEAUVOIR, *The Ethics of Ambiguity*, 1948

It is because there is true danger, true defeat, true damnation on this earth, that words of victory, wisdom, and joy have meaning.
—SIMONE DE BEAUVOIR, *The Ethics of Ambiguity*, 1, 1948

Existence is no more than the precarious attainment of relevance in an intensely mobile flux of past, present, and future.
—SUSAN SONTAG, *Styles of Radical Will,* "'Thinking Against Oneself': Reflections on Cioran," 1966

Life is a "zero-sum game"; we are gamblers playing with limited stakes against a house with infinite resources. We must eventually go under. We can only strive to hang on as long as possible, have some fun while we're at the table, and, since we happen to be moral agents as well, to stay the course with honor.
—STEPHEN JAY GOULD, "Staying the Course with Honor," in Fadiman, ed., *Living Philosophies,* 1990

The question of *the* meaning of life in general is meaningless because life has a meaning to anyone who has interest in it.
—SIDNEY HOOK, "It Didn't Have to Be," in Fadiman, ed., *Living Philosophies,* 1990

The Physical
&
Metaphysical

Nature

There is no need to show at length that Nature has no particular goal in view, and final causes are mere human figments.
—BENEDICT DE SPINOZA, *Ethics*, I, Appendix, 1677

The tree which moves some to tears of joy is in the Eyes of others only a Green thing that stands in the way. Some see Nature all Ridicule and Deformity . . . & Some Scarce see Nature at all, But to the Eyes of the Man of Imagination Nature is Imagination itself.
—WILLIAM BLAKE, letter to Trusler, August 23, 1799

I compare the earth and her atmosphere to a great living being perpetually inhaling and exhaling.
—JOHANN WOLFGANG VON GOETHE, *Conversations with Eckermann* (1836), April 11, 1827

Nature understands no jesting; she is always true, always serious, always severe. . . . The man incapable of appreciating her she

despises; and only to the apt, the pure, and the true does she resign herself, and reveal her secrets.
—JOHANN WOLFGANG VON GOETHE, *Conversations with Eckermann* (1836), February 13, 1829

Pervading all Nature we may see at work a stern discipline which is a little cruel that it may be very kind.
—HERBERT SPENCER, *Social Statics*, "Poor Laws," 1850

What a book a devil's chaplain might write on the clumsy, wasteful, blundering, low, and horribly cruel works of nature!
—CHARLES DARWIN, letter to Joseph Hooker, July 13, 1856

Nature has her language, and she is not unveracious; but we don't know all the intricacies of her syntax just yet, and in a hasty reading we may happen to extract the very opposite of her real meaning.
—GEORGE ELIOT, *Adam Bede*, 1859

Nature, so far as we can discern, without passion and without intention, forms, transforms, and retransforms forever. She neither weeps nor rejoices. She produces man without purpose, and obliterates him without regret.
—ROBERT G. INGERSOLL, *The Gods*, 1872

There are in nature neither rewards nor punishments – there are consequences.
—ROBERT G. INGERSOLL, *Some Reasons Why*, 1881

Natures teaches more than she preaches. There are no sermons in stones. It is easier to get a spark out of a stone than a moral.
—JOHN BURROUGHS, *Time and Change*, "The Gospel of Nature," 1912

Nature's way of dealing with unhealthy conditions is unfortunately not one that compels us to conduct a solvent hygiene on a cash basis. She demoralizes us with long credits and reckless overdrafts, and then pulls us up cruelly with catastrophic bankruptcies.
—GEORGE BERNARD SHAW, *Heartbreak House*, 1919

Nature holds no brief for the human experiment: it must stand or fall by its results. If Man will not serve, Nature will try another experiment.
—GEORGE BERNARD SHAW, *Back to Methuselah*, "Preface," 1921

Nature averages up well. We see nothing like purpose or will in her total scheme of things, yet inside her hit-and-miss methods, her storms and tornadoes and earthquakes and distempers, we see a fundamental benefaction.
—JOHN BURROUGHS, *The Last Harvest*, "A Critical Glance into Darwin," 1922

Nature conceals her secrets because she is sublime, not because she is a trickster.
—ALBERT EINSTEIN, scribbled aphorism, mid 20th century. Quoted in Calaprice, *The Quotable Einstein* (1996)

I have never imputed to Nature a purpose or a goal, or anything that could be understood as anthropomorphic. What I see in Nature is a magnificent structure that we can comprehend only very imperfectly, and that must fill a thinking person with a feeling of humility.
—ALBERT EINSTEIN, quoted statement, 1954 or 1955. Quoted in Dukas & Hoffmann, eds., *Albert Einstein: The Human Side* (1979)

We have agreed not to drive our automobiles into cathedrals, concert halls, art museums, legislative assemblies, private bedrooms, and other sanctums of our culture; we should treat our national parks with the same deference, for they, too, are holy places.
—EDWARD ABBEY, *Desert Solitaire*, "Polemic: Industrial Tourism and the National Parks," 1971

Nature is what she is – amoral and persistent.
—STEPHEN JAY GOULD, *New York Times*, May 6, 1979

Humanity's view of the world as *our* property, *our* dominion, *our* stewardship, is like that of a child who imagines himself as the center of existence, with all other beings having no purpose but to serve him.
—EDWARD ABBEY, *Confessions of a Barbarian*, December 15, 1989

Molecules don't have passports. All the creatures on Earth are in this together. We need a primary allegiance to the species and to planet Earth.
—CARL SAGAN, in Eknath Easwaran, *The Compassionate Universe*, 1989

Science

To command the professors of astronomy to confute their own observations is to enjoin an impossibility, for it is to command them to see what they do not see, and not to understand what they do understand, and to find what they do not discover.
—GALILEO GALILEI, letter to Christine, Grand Duchess of Tuscany: "The Authority of Scripture in Philosophical Controversies," 1615. Referring to the Church's coercive attempts to make Galileo disavow his discoveries

Diderot: Do you see this egg? With this you can topple every theological theory, every church or temple in the world.
—DENIS DIDEROT, *Conversation Between D'Alembert and Diderot* (1830), 1769

Science is the great antidote to the poison of enthusiasm and superstition.
—ADAM SMITH, *The Wealth of Nations*, V, 1, 3, 1776

Science is, I believe, nothing but *trained and organized common sense*, differing from the latter only as a veteran may differ from a raw recruit; and its methods differ from those of common sense only so far as the guardman's cut and thrust differ from the manner in which a savage wields his club.
—THOMAS H. HUXLEY, *Collected Essays*, Vol. III, "On the Educational Value of the Natural History Sciences," 1854

About thirty years ago there was much talk that geologists ought only to observe and not theorize. . . . How odd it is that anyone should not see that all observation must be for or against some view if it is to be of any service.

—CHARLES DARWIN, letter to Henry Fawcett, September 18, 1861

The man of science has learned to believe in justification, not by faith, but by verification.

—THOMAS H. HUXLEY, *Collected Essays*, Vol. I, "On the Advisableness of Improving Natural Knowledge," 1866

Science is a first-rate piece of furniture for a man's upper chamber, if he has common sense on the ground floor.

—OLIVER WENDELL HOLMES, *The Poet at the Breakfast Table*, 5, 1872

The sciences are not sectarian. People do not persecute each other on account of disagreements in mathematics. Families are not divided about botany, and astronomy does not even tend to make a man hate his father and mother. It is what people do not know that they persecute each other about.

—ROBERT G. INGERSOLL, *Some Mistakes of Moses*, 1879

The scientific spirit is of more value than its products, and irrationally held truths may be more harmful than reasoned errors.

—THOMAS H. HUXLEY, *Collected Essays*, Vol. II, "The Coming of Age of 'The Origin of Species,' " 1880

The Physical & Metaphysical

We have not the reverent feeling for the rainbow that a savage has, because we know how it is made. We have lost as much as we have gained by prying into that matter.
—MARK TWAIN, *A Tramp Abroad*, 14, 1880

Science may be regarded as a minimal problem consisting of the completest presentation of facts with the least possible expenditure of thought.
—ERNST MACH, *The Science of Mechanics*, IV, 4, 1883

There is no harmony between religion and science. When science was a child, religion sought to strangle it in the cradle. Now that science has attained its youth, and superstition is in its dotage, the trembling, palsied wreck says to the athlete: "Let us be friends." It reminds me of the bargain the cock wished to make with the horse: "Let us agree not to step on each other's feet."
—ROBERT G. INGERSOLL, interview in *The Truth Seeker*, September 5, 1885

A scientist in his laboratory is not only a technician. He is also a child placed before natural phenomena which impress him like a fairy tale.
—MARIE CURIE, quoted in Eve Curie, *Madame Curie* (1938), probably early 20th century

The defect of science is that it is inadequate or abstract, that the account it gives of things is not full and sensuous enough; but its merit is that, like sense, it makes external being present to a creature that is concerned in adjusting itself to its environment, and informs that creature about things other than itself.
—GEORGE SANTAYANA, *Reason in Science*, 1, 1906

Great Freethinkers

Science has fairly turned us out of our comfortable little anthropomorphic notion of things into the great out-of-doors of the
universe. We must and will get used to the chill.
—JOHN BURROUGHS, *Time and Change*, 'The Long Road," 1912

Humanity has in the course of time had to endure from the hands of
science two great outrages upon its self-love. The first was when it
realized that our earth was not the center of the universe. . . . The
second was when biological research robbed man of his peculiar privilege of having been specially created, and relegated him to descent
from the animal world. . . . But man's craving for grandiosity is now
suffering the third and most bitter blow from present day psychological research, which is endeavoring to prove to the ego in each one
of us that he is not even master in his own house.
—SIGMUND FREUD, *A General Introduction to Psychoanalysis*, 18, 1917

God give me unclouded eyes and freedom from haste. God give me
quiet and relentless anger against all pretense and all pretentious
work and all work left slack and unfinished. God give me a restlessness whereby I may neither sleep nor accept praise until my observed
results equal my calculated results, or, in pious glee, I discover and
assault my error. God give me strength not to trust to God.
—SINCLAIR LEWIS, *Arrowsmith*, 1925. Scientist's credo

Science can teach us, and I think our own hearts can teach us, no
longer to look around for imaginary supports, no longer to invent
allies in the sky, but rather to look to our own efforts here below to
make this world a fit place to live in.
—BERTRAND RUSSELL, *Why I Am Not a Christian* (1957), "Why I am
Not a Christian," 1927

The Physical & Metaphysical

There is nothing which a scientific mind would more regret than reaching a condition in which there were no more problems. That state would be the death of science, not its perfected life.
—JOHN DEWEY, *The Quest for Certainty*, 4, 1929

Concern for man himself and his fate must always be the chief interest of all technical endeavors . . . in order that the creations of our mind shall be a blessing and not a curse to mankind. Never forget this in the midst of your diagrams and equations.
—ALBERT EINSTEIN, address at the California Institute of Technology, *The New York Times*, February 17, 1931

If science is not to leave a gap which will inevitably be filled with superstition, man must learn to feel himself a citizen of the universe as depicted by science.
—J. B. S. HALDANE, *The Inequality of Man and Other Essays*, "What I think About," 1932

A *Weltanschauung* based upon science has, apart from the emphasis it lays upon the real world, essentially negative characteristics, such as that it limits itself to truth, and rejects illusions. Those of our fellow men who are dissatisfied with this state of things and who desire something more for their peace of mind may look for it where they can find it.
—SIGMUND FREUD, *New Introductory Lectures in Psychoanalysis*, 7, 1933

It would be a poor thing to be an atom in a universe without physicists. And physicists are made of atoms. A physicist is an atom's way of knowing about atoms.
—GEORGE WALD, "Foreward" to Henderson, *The Fitness of the Environment*, 1958

Science is the search for truth – it is not a game in which one tries to beat his opponent.
—LINUS PAULING, *No More War!* 1958

Science does not rest upon solid bedrock. The bold structure of its theories rises, as it were, above a swamp. It is like a building erected on piles. . . . If we stop driving the piles deeper, it is not because we have reached firm ground. We simply stop when we are satisfied that the piles are firm enough to carry the structure, at least for the time being.
—KARL POPPER, *The Logic of Scientific Discovery*, 1959

Irrefutability is not a virtue of a theory (as people often think) but a vice. . . . The criterion of the scientific status of a theory is its falsifiability, or refutability, or testability.
—KARL POPPER, *Conjectures and Refutations*, 1968

Objectivity is not an unobtainable emptying of mind, but a willingness to abandon a set of preferences . . . when the world seems to work in a contrary way.
—STEPHEN J. GOULD, *Dinosaur in a Haystack*, "Dinosaur in a Haystack," 1995

The ideal scientist thinks like a poet and works like a book-keeper.
—EDWARD O. WILSON, *Consilience*, 4, 1998

Matter. Materialism

Nothing can come into being from that which is not nor pass away into that which is not.
—DEMOCRITUS, quoted in Diogenes Laërtius, *Lives of Eminent Philosophers*, IX, 7, 5th–4th century B.C.

First-beginnings therefore are of solid singleness, massed together and cohering closely. . . . From them nature allows nothing to be torn, nothing further to be worn away, reserving them as seeds for things.
—LUCRETIUS, *On the Nature of Things*, I, ca. 50 B.C.

To talk of immaterial existences is to talk of nothings. To say that the human soul, angels, God, are immaterial, is to say they are nothings, or that there is no God, no angels, no soul. I cannot reason otherwise.
—THOMAS JEFFERSON, letter to John Adams, August 15, 1820

The chief defect of all hitherto existing materialism . . . is that the thing, reality, sensuousness, is conceived only in the form of the object or of contemplation, but not as human sensuous activity, practice.
—KARL MARX, *Theses on Feuerbach*, 1845

The materialist doctrine that men are products of circumstances and upbringing . . . forgets that it is men who change circumstances and that it is essential to educate the educator himself.
—KARL MARX, *Theses on Feuerbach*, 1845

Man is a machine into which we put what we call food, and produce what we call thought. Think of that wonderful chemistry by which bread was changed into the divine tragedy of *Hamlet!*
—ROBERT G. INGERSOLL, *The Gods*, 1872

If by spirit you mean that which thinks, then I am a believer in spirit. If you mean by spirit the something that says "I," the something that reasons, hopes, loves, and aspires, then I am a believer in spirit. Whatever spirit there is in the universe must be a natural thing, and not superimposed upon nature.
—ROBERT G. INGERSOLL, *My Reviewers Reviewed*, 1, 1877

Intellect and morals appear only the material forces on a higher plane. The laws of material nature run up into the invisible world of the mind, and hereby we acquire a key to those sublimities which skulk and hide in the caverns of human consciousness.
—RALPH WALDO EMERSON, *Lectures and Biographical Sketches*, "Perpetual Forces," 1884

Objects or things are no dead materials merely fit to be acted upon; matter is animated everywhere by forces. . . . Force and matter are inseparable.
—PAUL CARUS, *Monism and Meliorism*, "Definitions and Explanations," 1885

I make no claims for what is called the *spiritual* by the churches, formal penalistic arguers. Indeed, I am quite staggered, shocked, to have it attached to me. . . . *Leaves [of Grass]* . . . are bits out of life,

words, hints, coarse, direct, unmistakeable. . . . with the traces of their material origin clinging everywhere on them.
—WALT WHITMAN, quoted in Traubel, *Walt Whitman in Camden*, Vol. IX, October 20, 1891. Whitman's last recorded comments on matter and spirit

The true mystery of the world is the visible, not the invisible.
—OSCAR WILDE, *Picture of Dorian Gray*, 2, 1891

Metaphysicians, confounding dialectic with physics and thereby corrupting both, will discuss for ever the difference it makes to substance whether you call it matter or God.
—GEORGE SANTAYANA, *Reason in Science*, 7, 1906

If you are in the habit of believing in special providences, or of expecting to continue your romantic adventures in a second life, materialism will dash your hopes most unpleasantly, and you may think for a year or two that you have nothing to live for. But a thorough materialist, one born to the faith and not half plunged into it by an unexpected christening in cold water, will be like the superb Democritus, a laughing philosopher.
—GEORGE SANTAYANA, *Reason in Science*, 3, 1906

I do not know what matter is in itself: but what metaphysical idealists call spirit, if it is understood to be responsible for what goes on in the world and in myself, and to be the "reality" of these appearances, is, in respect to my spiritual existence, precisely what I call matter.
—GEORGE SANTAYANA, *Scepticism and Animal Faith*, 26, 1923

The theory of relativity, by merging time into space-time, has damaged the traditional notion of substance more than all the arguments of philosophers. . . . A piece of matter has become, not a persistent thing with varying states, but a system of inter-related events.
—BERTRAND RUSSELL, "Introduction" to Lange, *The History of Materialism*, 1925

It is not materialism that is the chief curse of the world, as pastors teach, but idealism. Men get into trouble by taking their visions and hallucinations too seriously.
—H. L. MENCKEN, *Minority Report*, 305, 1956

What do I believe in? I believe in sun. In rock. In the dogma of the sun and the doctrine of the rock. I believe in blood, fire, woman, rivers, eagles, storms, drums, flutes, banjos, and broom-tailed horses.
—EDWARD ABBEY, *A Voice Crying in the Wilderness*, 1989

Change. Evolution

There is nothing permanent except change.
—HERACLITUS, quoted in Diogenes Laërtius, *Lives of Eminent Philosophers*, IX, 1, 6th–5th century B.C.

It is not possible to step twice into the same river.
—HERACLITUS, Fragments (Freeman transl.), 6th–5th century B.C.

The Physical & Metaphysical

The first-beginnings of things were sorted out not through design and keen intelligence. . . . but because after shifting about in many ways throughout the universe they were driven and tormented by blows from limitless time.
—LUCRETIUS, *On the Nature of Things*, I, ca. 50 B.C.

Just as in the animal and vegetable kingdoms, an individual begins, grows, subsists, decays, and passes away, could it not be the same with whole species?
—DENIS DIDEROT, *Thoughts on the Interpretation of Nature*, 58, 1754

The result, therefore, of our present inquiry is, that we find no vestige of a beginning – no prospect of an end.
—JAMES HUTTON, *Theory of the Earth*, final sentence, 1788

There are no fixtures in nature. The universe is fluid and volatile. Permanence is but a word of degrees. Our globe seen by God is a transparent law, not a mass of facts. The law dissolves the fact and holds it fluid.
—RALPH WALDO EMERSON, *Essays*, First Series, "Circles," 1841

Variations, however slight and from whatever cause proceeding, if they be in any degree profitable to the individuals of a species, in their infinitely complex relations to other organic beings and to their physical conditions of life, will tend to the preservation of such individuals, and will generally be inherited by the offspring. . . . I have called this principle, by which each slight variation, if useful, is preserved, by the term Natural Selection.
—CHARLES DARWIN, *The Origin of Species*, 3, 1859

I certainly have more patience with those who trace mankind upward from a low condition, even from the lower animals, than with those who start him from a point of perfection and conduct him to a level with the brutes.

—FREDERICK DOUGLASS, letter quoted in Booker Washington, *Frederick Douglass* (1907), 1874

The more we learn of the nature of things, the more evident is it that what we call rest is only unperceived activity; that seeming peace is silent but strenuous battle. In every part, at every moment, the state of the cosmos is the expression of a transitory adjustment of contending forces.

—THOMAS H. HUXLEY, *Collected Essays*, Vol. IX, "Evolution and Ethics," 1893

Evolution is not an explanation of the cosmic process, but merely a generalized statement of the method and results of that process.

—THOMAS H. HUXLEY, *Collected Essays*, Vol. IX, "Evolution and Ethics: Prolegomena," 1894

The usual fate of a species in the past has not been progress, but extermination, very often after deteriorating slowly through long periods. . . . There is no reason to suppose that man will escape it unless he makes an effort to do so.

—J. B. S. HALDANE, *The Inequality of Man and Other Essays*, "Possibilities of Human Evolution," 1932

Man's most sacred duty, and at the same time his most glorious opportunity, is to promote the maximum fulfillment of the evolu-

tionary process on this earth; and this includes the fullest realization of his own inherent possibilities.
—JULIAN HUXLEY, *New Bottles for New Wine*, "Evolutionary Humanism," 1957

Natural selection, the blind, unconscious, automatic process which Darwin discovered . . . has no purpose in mind. It has no mind and no mind's eye. It does not plan for the future. It has no vision, no foresight, no sight at all. If it can be said to play the role of the watchmaker in nature, it is the *blind* watchmaker.
—RICHARD DAWKINS, *The Blind Watchmaker*, 1, 1986

Humans are not the end result of a predictable evolutionary process, but rather a fortuitous cosmic afterthought, a tiny little twig on the enormously arborescent bush of life, which, if replanted from seed, would almost surely not grow this twig again.
—STEPHEN J. GOULD, *Dinosaur in a Haystack*, "Can We Complete Darwin's Revolution?" 1995

Circumstance

Men have fashioned an image of chance as an excuse for their own stupidity. For Chance rarely conflicts with intelligence, and most things in life can be set in order by an intelligent sharpsightedness.
—DEMOCRITUS, Fragment (Freeman transl.), 5th–4th century B.C.

The more we amplify our needs and our possessions, the more we expose ourselves to the blows of fortune and adversity. The range of our desires should be circumscribed and confined to a narrow limit of the nearest advantages.
—MICHEL DE MONTAIGNE, *Essays*, III, 10, 1588

A change of fortune hurts a wise man no more than a change of the moon.
—BENJAMIN FRANKLIN, *Poor Richard's Almanac*, 1756

The first thing that strikes me on hearing a Misfortune having befallen another is this – "Well it cannot be helped: he will have the pleasure of trying the resources of his Spirit."
— JOHN KEATS, letter to Benjamin Bailey, November 22, 1817

You think me the child of my circumstances: I make my circumstance.
—RALPH WALDO EMERSON, *Nature; Addresses, and Lectures* (1849), "The Transcendentalist," 1842

We may regard the petty vexations of life that are constantly happening as designed to keep us in practice for bearing great misfortunes, so that we may not become completely enervated by a career of prosperity.
—ARTHUR SCHOPENHAUER, *Parerga and Paralipomena*, Vol. I, "Aphorisms on the Wisdom of Life," 5, 1851

The element running through entire nature, which we popularly call Fate, is known to us as limitation. Whatever limits us, we call Fate.
—RALPH WALDO EMERSON, *The Conduct of Life*, "Fate," 1860

'Tis the best use of Fate to teach a fatal courage. . . . For, if Fate is so prevailing, man also is part of it, and can confront fate with fate. If the Universe have these savage accidents, our atoms are as savage in resistance.
—RALPH WALDO EMERSON, *The Conduct of Life*, "Fate," 1860

Is not the 'aim,' the purpose, often enough only an extenuating pretext, an additional self-blinding of conceit, which does not wish to admit that the ship *follows* the stream into which it has accidentally run? That it "wishes" to go that way *because* it *must* go that way? That it has a direction, sure enough, but – not a steersman? We still require a criticism of the concept of "purpose."
—FRIEDRICH NIETZSCHE, *The Gay Science*, 360, 1882

Let accidents come to me, they are innocent as little children.
—FRIEDRICH NIETZSCHE, *Thus Spoke Zarathustra* (Kaufmann transl.), III, 6, 1884

My formula for the greatness of a human being is *amor fati* [love of fate]: that one should wish to have nothing altered – either in the future, the past, or for all eternity. Not merely bear what is necessary, still less hide it . . . but *love* it.
—FRIEDRICH NIETZSCHE, *Ecce Homo*, "Why I Am So Clever," 10, 1888

Chance is perhaps the pseudonym of God when He did not want to sign.
—ANATOLE FRANCE, *Le Jardin d'Épicure*, 1894

Great Freethinkers

We are like billiard balls in a game played by unskilled players, continually being nearly sent into a pocket, but hardly ever getting right into it, except by a fluke.
—SAMUEL BUTLER, *Note-Books* (1912), 1, late 19th century

It's no use crying over spilt milk, because all the forces of the universe were bent on spilling it.
—W. SOMERSET MAUGHAM, *Of Human Bondage*, 67, 1915

Failure or success seem to have been allotted to men by their stars. But they retain the power of wriggling, of fighting with their star or against it, and in the whole universe the only interesting movement is this wriggle.
—E. M. FORSTER, *Abinger Harvest*, "Our Diversions," 1936

Those who didn't share in the good fortune of the mighty often share in their misfortune.
—BERTOLT BRECHT, *The Caucasian Chalk-Circle*, I, 1949

It is important to be able to view human beings as products of circumstances. . . . It is a waste of energy to be angry with a man who behaves badly: just as it is to be angry with a car that won't go.
—BERTRAND RUSSELL, *The Art of Philosophizing*, 1, 1968

Aging

There is an intelligence of the young, and an unintelligence of the aged. It is not time that teaches wisdom, but early training and natural endowment.
—DEMOCRITUS, Fragment (Freeman transl.), 5th-4th century B.C.

It would be a fine thing to be old if we only progressed toward improvement. It is the movement of a drunkard, staggering, dizzy, uncertain, or that of reeds stirred by the wind as it pleases.
—MICHEL DE MONTAIGNE, *Essays*, III, 9, 1588

When we are led by Nature's hand down a gentle and virtually imperceptible slope, bit by bit, one step at a time, she rolls us into this wretched state and makes us familiar with it; so that we feel no shock when youth dies within us, which in essence and in truth is a harder death than the complete death of a languishing life or the death of old age.
—MICHEL DE MONTAIGNE, *Essays* (Frame transl.), I, 20, 1580

People always fancy that we must become old to become wise; but, in truth, as years advance, it is hard to keep ourselves as wise as we were.
—JOHANN WOLFGANG VON GOETHE, *Conversations with Eckermann* (1836), February 17, 1831

The first forty years of life furnish the text, while the remaining thirty supply the commentary.
—ARTHUR SCHOPENHAUER, *Parerga and Paralipomena*, Vol. I, "Aphorisms on the Wisdom of Life," 6, 1851

The youth gets together his materials to build a bridge to the moon, or, perchance, a palace or temple on the earth, and, at length, the middle-aged man concludes to build a woodshed with them.
—HENRY DAVID THOREAU, *Journal*, July 14, 1852

Measure your health by your sympathy with morning and spring. If there is no response in you to the awakening of nature, if the prospect of an early morning walk does not banish sleep, if the warble of the first bluebird does not thrill you, know that the morning and spring of your life are past. Thus may you feel your pulse.
—HENRY DAVID THOREAU, *Journal*, February 25, 1859

After a while the fires of life begin to smoulder; the ashes accumulate. Then some mild excitement is needed, some social stimulus, something to fan the coals a little.
—JOHN BURROUGHS, *Journal*, November, 1899. Quoted in Barrus, *The Life and Letters of John Burroughs* (1925)

At times it seems that I am living my life backward, and that at the approach of old age my real youth will begin. My soul was born covered with wrinkles – wrinkles that my ancestors and parents most assiduously put there and that I had the greatest trouble removing, in some cases.
—ANDRÉ GIDE, *Pretexts*, 1903

The Physical & Metaphysical

Use your health, even to the point of wearing it out. That is what it is for. Spend all you have before you die; and do not outlive yourself.
—GEORGE BERNARD SHAW, *Doctor's Dilemma*, "Preface on Doctors," 1911

Old men cherish a fond delusion that there is something mystically valuable in mere quantity of experience. Now the fact is, of course, that it is the young people who have all the really valuable experience. . . . It is only the interpretation of this first collision with life that is worth anything.
—RANDOLPH BOURNE, *Youth and Life*, "Youth," 1913

The man who has reached the age of thirty-six has just about achieved readiness to discard the illusions built on the false theories for which wrong instruction and youthful ignorance previously have made him an easy mark. He is just beginning to get down to business.
—THOMAS A. EDISON, *The Diary and Sundry Observations* (1948), 1927

Old age is similar to death in that some people confront it with indifference, not because they have more courage than others, but because they have less imagination.
—MARCEL PROUST, *Le temps retrouvé*, "Matinée chez la princesse de Guermantes," 1927

There is, after all, something eternal that lies beyond the reach of the hand of fate and of all human delusions. And such eternals lie closer to an older person than to a younger one who oscillates between fear and hope.
—ALBERT EINSTEIN, letter to Queen Elizabeth of Belgium, March 20, 1936. Quoted in Calaprice, *The Quotable Einstein* (1996)

I live in that solitude which is painful in youth, but delicious in the years of maturity.
—ALBERT EINSTEIN, *Out of My Later Years* (1950), "Self-Portrait," 1936

We do not grow absolutely, chronologically. We grow sometimes in one dimension, and not in another, unevenly. We grow partially. We are relative. We are mature in one realm, childish in another. The past, present, and future mingle and pull us backward, forward, or fix us in the present.
—ANAÏS NIN, *The Diary of Anaïs Nin*, Vol. IV (1971), 1946

What is an adult? A child puffed up with age.
—SIMONE DE BEAUVOIR, *La Femme rompue, L'âge de discrétion*, 1967

The nearer I come to the end of my days, the more I am enabled to see that strange thing, a life, and to see it whole.
—SIMONE DE BEAUVOIR, *All Said and Done*, 1972

Death

To fear death is only to think ourselves wise without really being wise, for it is to think that we know what we do not know. For no one knows whether death may not be the greatest good that can happen to man. But men fear it as if they knew quite well that it was the greatest of evils.
—SOCRATES, quoted in Plato's *Apology* (Church transl.), 4th century B.C.

For there is nothing terrible in life for the man who has truly comprehended that there is nothing terrible in not living. So that the man speaks but idly who says that he fears death, . . . since it is painful only in anticipation.
—EPICURUS, *Letter to Menoeceus*, 4th–3rd century B.C.

Thus the sum of things is ever renewed. . . . Some nations wax, others wane, and in a brief space the races of living things are changed and like runners hand over the lamp of life.
—LUCRETIUS, *On the Nature of Things*, II, ca. 50 B.C.

Why is it, mortal, that you indulge in excessive grief? Why shed tears that you must die? For if the life that is past has been one of enjoyment, and if all your pleasures have not passed through your mind as through a sieve . . . why then do you not, like a thankful guest, rise cheerfully from life's feast, and with a quiet mind go take your rest?
—LUCRETIUS, *On the Nature of Things*, III, ca. 50 B.C.

Speculation on death brings upon us many times greater pain than that which is to be expected. The man who imagines death, and is afraid of it, dies a separate death at every image he calls up.
—RHAZES, *The Spiritual Physick of Rhazes*, 20, ca. 900

Let us deprive it of its unfamiliarity, let us live with it, let us habituate ourselves to it; let us think of nothing so often as of death, let us constantly place it before our imaginations and in all its aspects; at the stumbling of a horse, at the fall of a tile, at the slightest prick of a pin, let us immediately reflect: Well, what if this were death itself? and thereupon let us stiffen and strengthen ourselves.
—MICHEL DE MONTAIGNE, *Essays* (Ives transl.), I, 20, 1580

If you do not know how to die, do not be concerned; Nature will instruct you on the spot, plainly and adequately. She will do this business perfectly for you; do not give it your attention.
—MICHEL DE MONTAIGNE, *Essays*, III, 12, 1588

Nothing is so horrifying as the possibility of existing simply because we do not know how to die.
—GERMAINE DE STÄEL, *The Influence of the Passions*, "On Philosophy," 1796

There is a ripeness of time for death . . . when it is reasonable we should drop off, and make room for another growth. When we have lived our generation out, we should not wish to encroach on another.
—THOMAS JEFFERSON, letter to John Adams, August 1, 1816

Animals learn death first in the moment of death; man proceeds onward with the knowledge that he is every hour approaching nearer to death, and this throws a feeling of uncertainty over life, even to the man who forgets in the busy scenes of life that annihilation is awaiting him. It is for this reason chiefly that we have philosophies and religions.
—ARTHUR SCHOPENHAUER, *The World as Will and Idea*, Book I, 8, 1819

The only poetic fact in the life of thousands and thousands is their death.
—RALPH WALDO EMERSON, *Journals*, August, 1842

The Physical & Metaphysical

It is sweet to think that I will serve one day to make the tulips grow. Who knows! The tree next to which I am laid will maybe produce excellent fruits; I will perhaps be splendid fertilizer, a superior guano.
—GUSTAVE FLAUBERT, letter to Louise Colet, August 26, 1846

To love everything and everybody and always to sacrifice oneself for love meant not to love anyone, not to live this earthly life. And the more imbued he became with that principle of love, the more he renounced life and the more completely he destroyed that dreadful barrier which . . . stands between life and death.
—LEO TOLSTOY, *War and Peace*, XII, 4, 1862. Referring to the mortally wounded Prince Andrew Bolkanski

In certain cases it is indecent to go on living. To continue to vegetate in a state of cowardly dependence upon doctors, once the meaning of life has been lost, ought to be regarded with the greatest contempt of mankind.
—FRIEDRICH NIETZSCHE, *Twilight of the Idols*, "Skirmishes of an Untimely Man," 36, 1889

To die in a dignified manner when it is no longer possible to live in a dignified manner; death voluntarily chosen, death at the right time, carried out brightly and cheerfully in the midst of children and witnesses: then a true farewell is still possible.
—FRIEDRICH NIETZSCHE, *Twilight of the Idols*, "Skirmishes of an Untimely Man," 36, 1889

We are all sentenced to capital punishment for the crime of living.
—OLIVER WENDELL HOLMES, *Over the Teacups*, 1891

Love makes us poets, and the approach of death should make us philosophers.
—GEORGE SANTAYANA, *The Sense of Beauty*, IV, 59, 1896

I have wrestled with death. It is the most unexciting contest you can imagine. It takes place in an impalpable greyness, with nothing underfoot, with nothing around, without spectators, without clamour, without glory, without the great desire for victory, without the great fear of defeat.
—JOSEPH CONRAD, Marlow in *Heart of Darkness*, 1902

We need not wait for our total death to experience dying. . . . Every moment celebrates obsequies over the virtues of its predecessor; and the possession of memory, by which we somehow survive in representation, is the most unmistakable proof that we are perishing in reality. In endowing us with memory, nature has revealed to us a truth utterly unimaginable to the unreflective creation, the truth of mortality.
—GEORGE SANTAYANA, *Reason in Religion*, 14, 1905

Death is for many of us the gate of hell; but we are inside on the way out, not outside on the way in.
—GEORGE BERNARD SHAW, *Misalliance*, "Preface," 1914

I feel myself so much a part of everything living that I am not in the least concerned with the beginning or ending of the concrete existence of any one person in this eternal flow.
—ALBERT EINSTEIN, letter to Hedwig Born, April 18, 1920. Quoted in Calaprice, *The Quotable Einstein* (1996)

The Physical & Metaphysical

That the end of life should be death may sound sad: yet what other end can anything have? The end of an evening party is to go to bed; but its use is to gather congenial people together, that they may pass the time pleasantly. . . . The transitoriness of things is essential to their physical being, and not at all sad in itself; it becomes sad by virtue of a sentimental illusion.
—GEORGE SANTAYANA, *Some Turns of Thought in Modern Philosophy*, 4, 1933

Perhaps the whole root of our trouble, the human trouble, is that we will sacrifice all the beauty of our lives, will imprison ourselves in totems, crosses, blood sacrifices, steeples, mosques, races, armies, flags, nations, in order to deny the fact of death, which is the only fact we have.
—JAMES BALDWIN, *The Fire Next Time*, "Letter from a Region in My Mind," 1963

Death not merely ends life, it also bestows upon it a silent completeness, snatched from the hazardous flux to which all things human are subject.
—HANNAH ARENDT, *The Life of the Mind*, Vol. I, 16, 1978

*   *   *   *   *

Give the boys a holiday.
—ANAXAGORAS, last words of this philosopher and school master when asked if he wished for anything, 5th century B.C.

Now, farewell. Remember all my words.
—EPICURUS, words spoken while taking leave of his disciples for the last time, 270 B.C.

Now I am about to take my last voyage, a great leap in the dark.
—THOMAS HOBBES, final comment, 1679

Let me die in peace!
—VOLTAIRE, words spoken when a priest was called in to administer the last rites, 1778

I have no wish to believe on that subject.
—THOMAS PAINE, death bed words when asked by a friend if he wished to believe that Jesus Christ was the Son of God, 1809

I'll sleep as soundly as any old peasant woman.
—GERMAINE DE STÄEL, last words when asked if she was ready to sleep after receiving a dose of opium, 1817

Open the shutter in the bedroom so that more light can come in.
—JOHANN WOLFGANG VON GOETHE, request to his valet just prior to death, 1832

One world at a time.
—HENRY DAVID THOREAU, words shortly before his death to Parker Pillsbury who wished to discuss the next life. Reported in F.B. Sanborn, *Henry D. Thoreau* (1882), 1862

It took nature a long time to do her work, but I am almost out of the world.
—HENRY DAVID THOREAU, words to Bronson Alcott on his final day, 1862

Oh, if I get well, I will do wonderful things! My mind is bubbling with ideas!
—EUGÈNE DELACROIX, last words, 1863

I have had an outstanding portion of life, and I do not ask for any other life. I see no reason why the existence of Harriet Martineau should be perpetuated.
—HARRIET MARTINEAU, last words, 1876

So, this is death! Well. . . .
—THOMAS CARLYLE, last words, 1881

My dear Schur, you certainly remember our first talk. You promised me then not to forget me when my time comes. Now it's nothing but torture and makes no sense anymore. I thank you. Tell Anna about this.
—SIGMUND FREUD, instructions to his doctor, Max Schur, on his last day. Schur administered an overdose of painkillers to Freud the following day as he had requested, 1939

Yes, my friend. But my anguish is entirely physical. There are no more difficulties whatsoever.
—GEORGE SANTAYANA, final words when asked if he was suffering, 1952

If only I had more mathematics!
—ALBERT EINSTEIN, to his son the night before his death, 1955

I have finished my task here.

—ALBERT EINSTEIN, said as he was dying, 1955. Quoted in Calaprice, *The Quotable Einstein* (1996)

I did what I could.

—EDWARD ABBEY, last words, 1989

The Arts

Aesthetics

Poets [should] talk always of eternity, infinity, immensity, time, space, divinity, tombs, . . . hell, dark skies, deep seas, dim forests, thunder, flashes rending the clouds. Be dark.
—DENIS DIDEROT, *Salon of 1767* (1798), 1767

The conflict of good and evil cannot be aesthetically represented, for something has to be added to evil and taken from good to bring them into a state of balance.
—JOHANN WOLFGANG VON GOETHE, *Notes for the Autobiography*, 7, ca. 1814

We hate poetry that has a palpable design upon us. . . . Poetry should be great and unobtrusive, a thing which enters into one's soul, and does not startle it or amaze it with itself, but with its subject.
—JOHN KEATS, letter to John Reynolds, February 3, 1818

I am rather of the opinion that the more incommensurable, and the more incomprehensible to the understanding, a poetic production is, so much the better it is.

—JOHANN WOLFGANG VON GOETHE, *Conversations with Eckermann* (1836), May 6, 1827

Life is never beautiful, but only the pictures of life are so in the transfiguring mirror of art or of poetry.

—ARTHUR SCHOPENHAUER, *The World as Will and Idea*, Supplements to Book III, 30, 1844

Art for me . . . is a negation of society, an affirmation of the individual, outside of all the rules and all the demands of society.

—ÉMILE ZOLA, *Mes Haines*, 1866

It is one of the great privileges of Art that the horrible, artistically expressed, becomes beauty, and that sorrow, cadenced and harmonized, fills the spirit with a calm joy.

—CHARLES BAUDELAIRE, *L'Art Romantique*, "Théophile Gautier," 1868

In matters of art I confess that I do not hate excess; moderation never seemed to me to be a sign of an artistically vigorous nature. I like these excesses of health, these outbreaks of will, which inscribe themselves in works like inflamed asphalt in the heart of a volcano.

—CHARLES BAUDELAIRE, *L'Art Romantique*, "Richard Wagner," 1868

Nature, true Nature, and the true idea of Nature, long absent, must, above all, become fully restored, enlarged, and must furnish the

pervading atmosphere to poems. . . . I do not mean the smooth walks, trimm'd hedges, poseys and nightingales of the English poets, but the whole orb, with its geologic history, the kosmos, carrying fire and snow, that rolls through the illimitable areas, light as a feather, though weighing billions of tons.
—WALT WHITMAN, *Democratic Vistas*, 1871

Any art which professes to be founded on the special education or refinement of a limited body or class must of necessity be unreal and short-lived.
—WILLIAM MORRIS, "Art under Plutocracy," lecture delivered November 14, 1883

Art reminds us of states of animal vigor; it is . . . an excess and over-flow of blooming physicality into the world of images and desires.
—FRIEDRICH NIETZSCHE, *The Will to Power* (Kaufmann transl.), 802, 1887

The aesthetic principles are at bottom such axioms as that a note sounds good with its third and fifth, or that potatoes need salt.
—WILLIAM JAMES, *The Principles of Psychology*, 28, 1890

All bad poetry springs from genuine feeling. To be natural is to be obvious, and to be obvious is to be inartistic.
—OSCAR WILDE, *Intentions*, "The Critic as Artist," 1891

Art is Individualism, and Individualism is a disturbing and disinte-grating force. Therein lies its immense value. For what it seeks to

disturb is monotony of type, slavery of custom, tyranny of habit, and the reduction of man to the level of a machine.
—OSCAR WILDE, "The Soul of Man under Socialism," *Fortnightly Review*, February, 1891

Art is our spirited protest, our gallant attempt to teach Nature her proper place.
—OSCAR WILDE, *Intentions*, "The Decay of Lying," 1891

There is no such thing as a moral or an immoral book. Books are well written, or badly written. That is all.
—OSCAR WILDE, *The Picture of Dorian Gray*, "Preface," 1891

The most beautiful things are those that madness prompts and reason writes.
—ANDRÉ GIDE, *Journal*, September, 1894

The artist's rule must be Cromwell's: "Not what they want, but what is good for them."
—GEORGE BERNARD SHAW, "Two Bad Plays" in Dukore, ed., *The Drama Observed* (1993), 1895

Art itself may be defined as a single-minded attempt to render the highest kind of justice to the physical universe, by bringing to light the truth, manifold and one, underlying its every aspect.
—JOSEPH CONRAD, *The Nigger of the "Narcissus,"* "Preface," 1897

The artist appeals to the part of our being which is not dependent on wisdom; to that in us which is a gift and not an acquisition – and

therefore, more permanently enduring. He speaks to our capacity for delight and wonder.
—JOSEPH CONRAD, *The Nigger of the "Narcissus,"* "Preface," 1897

I don't know anything that mars good literature so completely as too much truth.
—MARK TWAIN, *Mark Twain's Speeches*, "The Savage Club Dinner," 1910

Poetry represents imagination's bold effort to escape from the cold and clammy facts that hedge us in.
—H. L. MENCKEN, *Prejudices*, Third Series, 1922

The essential function of art is moral. But a passionate, implicit morality, not didactic. A morality which changes the blood, rather than the mind. Changes the blood first. The mind follows later, in the wake.
—D. H. LAWRENCE, *Studies in Classic American Literature*, "Whitman," 1923

"The proper stuff of fiction" does not exist; everything is the proper stuff of fiction, every feeling, every thought; every quality of brain and spirit is drawn upon; no perception comes amiss.
—VIRGINIA WOOLF, *The Common Reader*, First Series, "Modern Fiction," 1925

An art work in which there are theories is like an object on which one has left the price mark.
—MARCEL PROUST, *Le temps retrouvé*, "Matinée chez la princesse de Guermantes," 1927

Fiction, imaginative work that is, is not dropped like a pebble upon the ground, as science may be; fiction is like a spider's web, attached ever so lightly perhaps, but still attached to life at all four corners.
—VIRGINIA WOOLF, *A Room of One's Own*, 3, 1929

The beauty of the world . . . has two edges, one of laughter, one of anguish, cutting the heart asunder.
—VIRGINIA WOOLF, *A Room of One's Own*, 1, 1929

The norms of classical art are the typical patterns of order, proportion, symmetry, equilibrium, harmony, and of all static and inorganic qualities. They are intellectual concepts which control or repress the vital instincts on which growth and therefore change depend.
—HERBERT READ, *Surrealism*, 1936

I hate that aesthetic game of the eye and the mind, played by these connoisseurs, these mandarins who "appreciate" beauty. What *is* beauty, anyway? There's no such thing. I never "appreciate," any more than I "like." I love or I hate.
—PABLO PICASSO, quoted in Gilot & Lake, *Life with Picasso* (1964), mid 20th century

Art is not and never has been subordinate to moral values. . . . Morality seeks to restrain the feelings; art seeks to define them by externalizing them, by giving them significant form.
—HERBERT READ, *The Realist Heresy*, 1953

Art is an indecent exposure of the consciousness.
—HERBERT READ, *The Realist Heresy*, 1953

By getting us used to what, formerly, we could not bear to see or hear, because it was too shocking, painful, or embarrassing, art changes morals.
—SUSAN SONTAG, *On Photography*, 1977

The Artist. Creativity

The great artist feels always the real imperfection of his own best works, and is more sensible than any man how much they fall short of that ideal perfection of which he has formed some conception. . . . It is the inferior artist only who is ever perfectly satisfied with his own performances.
—ADAM SMITH, *The Theory of Moral Sentiments*, VI, 3, 1759

Everyone is a genius at least once a year. The real geniuses simply have their bright ideas closer together.
—GEORG CHRISTOF LICHTENBERG, *Aphorisms*, in Mautner & Hatfield, eds., *The Lichtenberg Reader* (1959), 1779-88

A Poet is the most unpoetical of any thing in existence, because he has no Identity – he is continually in for and filling some other Body.
—JOHN KEATS, letter to R. Woodhouse, October 27, 1818

The only means of strengthening one's intellect is to make up one's mind about nothing – to let the mind be a thoroughfare for all thoughts, not a select party.
— JOHN KEATS, letter to George Keats, September, 1819

In your own Bosom you bear your Heaven and Earth, & all you behold; tho it appears Without, it is Within in your Imagination of which this World of Mortality is but a Shadow.
— WILLIAM BLAKE, *Jerusalem*, 71, ca. 1820

No rules for the great spirits; they are for people who have only talent which has been acquired.
—EUGÈNE DELACROIX, *Journal*, April 27, 1824

I notice that my spirit is never more excited to create than when it sees a mediocre production on a subject which suits me.
—EUGÈNE DELACROIX, *Journal*, April 27, 1824

A man is a poet who lives . . . by watching his moods. An old poet comes at last to watching his moods as narrowly as a cat does a mouse.
—HENRY DAVID THOREAU, *Journal*, August 28, 1851

There is no way to success in art but to take off your coat, grind paint, and work like a digger on the railroad, all day and every day.
—RALPH WALDO EMERSON, *Conduct of Life*, "Power," 1860

Would it not be easy to prove, through a philosophic comparison between the works of a mature artist and the state of his soul when he was a child, that genius is only childhood clearly formulated, endowed now with virile and powerful organs for expressing itself.
—CHARLES BAUDELAIRE, *Les Paradis artificiels*, "Un mangeur d'opium," 6, 1860

The Arts

A real painter regards with pleasure a well constructed arm with vigorous muscles even when it is used to beat a man to death. A true novelist enjoys contemplating the greatness of a mean sentiment or the ordered movements of a malicious character.
—HIPPOLYTE TAINE, *The History of English Literature*, "Introduction," 1863

A novelist, in my opinion, *has no right* to give his opinion on the things of this world. He is obliged in his vocation to imitate God in his, that is, to create and be silent.
—GUSTAVE FLAUBERT, letter to Mlle. Bosquet, August 20, 1866

To be a poet is to have a soul so quick to discern, that no shade of quality escapes it, and so quick to feel, that discernment is but a hand playing . . . on the chords of emotion: a soul in which knowledge passes instantaneously into feeling, and feeling flashes back as a new organ of knowledge.
—GEORGE ELIOT, *Middlemarch*, 22, 1871-2

Artists must be sacrificed to their art. Like bees, they must put their lives into the sting they give.
—RALPH WALDO EMERSON, *Letters and Social Aims*, "Inspiration," 1876

Here is a principle of aesthetics . . . , a rule for artists: Be well regulated in your life and ordinary like a bourgeois, in order to be violent and original in your works.
—GUSTAVE FLAUBERT, letter to Mme. Tennant, Christmas, 1876

Art is man's expression of his joy in labour.
—WILLIAM MORRIS, "Art under Plutocracy," lecture delivered
November 14, 1883

One must yet have chaos in oneself to be able to give birth to a
dancing star.
—FRIEDRICH NIETZSCHE, *Thus Spoke Zarathustra*, "Prologue," 5,
1883

Demoniac possession is mythical; but the faculty of being possessed,
more or less completely, by an idea is probably the fundamental
condition of what is called genius, whether it show itself in the saint,
the artist, or the man of science. . . . The concentration of all the rays
of intellectual energy on some one point, until it glows and colours
the whole cast of thought with its peculiar light, is common to all.
—THOMAS H. HUXLEY, *Collected Essays*, Vol. V, "An Episcopal
Trilogy," 1887

In order that there be art, in order that there be any aesthetic doing
and seeing, one physiological requirement is indispensable: intoxication [Rausch]. Intoxication must first have heightened the
excitability of the whole machine; otherwise there is no art.
—FRIEDRICH NIETZSCHE, *Twilight of the Idols*, "Skirmishes of an
Untimely Man," 8, 1889

My soul was the open inn at the crossroads; that which wished to
enter entered. I made myself ductile, conciliatory; I was at the
disposal of each one of my senses, attentive, a listener without a
single thought of himself.
—ANDRÉ GIDE, *Fruits of the Earth*, IV, 1, 1897

The artist, like the God of the creation, remains within or behind or beyond or above his handiwork, invisible, refined out of existence, indifferent, paring his fingernails.
—JAMES JOYCE, *Portrait of the Artist as a Young Man*, 5, 1916

All that is great comes to us from neurotics. It is they alone who have founded religions and created masterpieces. Never will the world know all that it owes to them and all that they have suffered to benefit us. We experience fine music, beautiful paintings, a thousand delicacies, but we do not know what they have cost those who have created them in terms of insomnia, tears, convulsive laughter, hives, asthma, epilepsy, and the fear of death, which is worse than everything else.
—MARCEL PROUST, *Le côte de Guermantes*, I, 1, 1920-1

A man of genius makes no mistakes. His errors are volitional and are the portals of discovery.
—JAMES JOYCE, *Ulysses*, 9, 1922

Masterpieces are not single and solitary births; they are the outcome of many years of thinking in common, of thinking by the body of the people, so that the experience of the mass is behind the single voice.
—VIRGINIA WOOLF, *A Room of One's Own*, 4, 1929

Perhaps a mind that is purely masculine cannot create, any more than a mind that is purely feminine. . . . It is fatal for anyone who writes to think of their sex. It is fatal to be a man or woman pure and simple; one must be woman-manly or man-womanly.
—VIRGINIA WOOLF, *A Room of One's Own*, 6, 1929

The knowing eye watches sharp as a needle; but the picture comes clean out of instinct, intuition, and sheer physical action. Once the instinct and intuition gets into the brush-tip, the picture *happens*, if it is to be a picture at all.
—D. H. LAWRENCE, *Assorted Articles*, "Making Pictures," 1930

Odd how the creative power at once brings the whole universe to order.
—VIRGINIA WOOLF, *A Writer's Diary*, July 27, 1934

It takes a lot of time to be a genius, you have to sit around so much doing nothing, really doing nothing.
—GERTRUDE STEIN, *Everybody's Autobiography*, 2, 1937

The artist is the opposite of the politically-minded individual, the opposite of the reformer, the opposite of the idealist. The artist does not tinker with the universe: he recreates it out of his own experience and understanding of life.
—HENRY MILLER, *The Cosmological Eye*, "An Open Letter to Surrealists Everywhere," 1939

Creating is living doubly.
—ALBERT CAMUS, *The Myth of Sisyphus*, "Absurd Creation," 1942

In order for the artist to have a world to express, he must first be situated in this world, oppressed or oppressing, resigned or rebellious, a man among men.
—SIMONE DE BEAUVOIR, *The Ethics of Ambiguity*, 1, 1948

If we could only pull out our brain and use only our eyes.
—PABLO PICASSO, quoted in Soby, J., "Afternoon with Picasso," *Saturday Review*, September 1, 1956

The Arts

Art lives only on the restraints it imposes on itself, and dies of all others.
—ALBERT CAMUS, *Resistance, Rebellion, and Death* (1961), "Create Dangerously," 1957

The most essential gift for a good writer is a built-in, shock-proof, shit detector. This is the writer's radar and all great writers have had it.
—ERNEST HEMINGWAY, interview in *Paris Review*, spring, 1958

In the creation of a work of art the artist is going through the exercise of attending to something quite particular other than himself. The intensity of this exercise gives to the work of art its special independence. . . . which is essentially the same as that conferred upon, or rather discovered in, another human being whom we love.
—IRIS MURDOCH, *Existentialists and Mystics* (1997), "The Sublime and the Good," 1959

Writers are specialized cells in the social organism. They are evolutionary cells. Mankind is trying to become something else; it's experimenting with new ideas all the time. And writers are a means of introducing new ideas into the society.
—KURT VONNEGUT, *Wampeters, Foma, and Granfalloons*, "Playboy Interview," 1974

Books choose their authors; the act of creation is not entirely a rational and conscious one.
—SALMAN RUSHDIE, *Independent on Sunday*, February 4, 1990

Language

The speech that I like is simple and natural speech, the same on paper as on the lips: a succulent, nervous, short, and concise manner of speaking, not dainty and nicely combed so much as vehement and brisk.
—MICHEL DE MONTAIGNE, *Essays* (Trechmann transl.), I, 26, 1580

Words are wise men's counters, they do but reckon by them; but they are the money of fools that value them by the authority of an Aristotle, a Cicero, or a Thomas [Aquinas], or any other doctor whatsoever, if but a man.
—THOMAS HOBBES, *Leviathan*, I, 4, 1651

I shall disdain to cull my phrases or polish my style . . . wishing rather to persuade by the force of my arguments than dazzle by the elegance of my language.
—MARY WOLLSTONECRAFT, *A Vindication of the Rights of Woman*, "Introduction," 1792

All symbols are fluxional; all language is vehicular and transitive, and is good, as ferries and horses are, for conveyance, not as farms and houses are, for homestead.
—RALPH WALDO EMERSON, *Essays*, Second Series, "The Poet," 1844

We cannot write well or truly but what we write with gusto. The body, the senses, must conspire with the mind. Expression is the act of the whole man, that our speech may be vascular.
—HENRY DAVID THOREAU, *Journal*, September 2, 1851

Authors should use common words to say uncommon things. But they do just the opposite. We find them trying to wrap up trivial ideas in grand words. . . . Their sentences perpetually stalk about on stilts.
—ARTHUR SCHOPENHAUER, *Parerga and Paralipomena*, Vol. II, 23, 1851

I would never use a long word where a short one would answer the purpose. I know there are professors in the country who "ligate" arteries. Other surgeons only tie them, and it stops the bleeding just as well.
—OLIVER WENDELL HOLMES, *Teaching from the Chair and at the Bedside*, 1867

This constitutes style: to have a refined and passionate soul, capable of irony, enthusiasm, hatred, admiration, to pass in the course of one page through twenty shades of emotion, to put fifty different intonations into fifty succeeding sentences and to transfer those successive states exactly into the reader's mind.
—HIPPOLYTE TAINE, "Notes on Germany," May 10, 1870. Quoted in *Life and Letters of Taine* (1904), Vol. II

We see, fore-indicated, amid these prospects and hopes . . . a language fann'd by the breath of Nature, which leaps overhead, cares mostly for impetus and effects, and for what it plants and invigorates to grow – tallies life and character, and seldomer tells a thing than suggests or necessitates it.
—WALT WHITMAN, *Democratic Vistas*, 1871

Most thinkers write badly because they communicate not only their thoughts but also the thinking of their thoughts.
—FRIEDRICH NIETZSCHE, *Human, All Too Human* (Hollingdale transl.), 188, 1878

Compact, severe, with as much substance as possible, a cold sarcasm against "beautiful words" and "beautiful sentiments" – here I found myself.
—FRIEDRICH NIETZSCHE, *Twilight of the Idols* (Kaufmann transl.), "What I Owe to the Ancients," 1, 1889

Pride of style in writing is just as bad as pride of style in dress, or equipage. The best style is the absence of style, or of all conscious style.
—JOHN BURROUGHS, *Journal*, summer, 1892. Quoted in Barrus, *The Life and Letters of John Burroughs* (1925)

Speech is an old torn net, through which the fish escape as one casts it over them.
—VIRGINIA WOOLF, "The Evening Party," 1918, in Dick, ed., *The Complete Shorter Fiction of Virginia Woolf*

For the essence of a sound style is that it cannot be reduced to rules, that it is a living and breathing thing with something of the demoniacal in it, that it fits its proprietor tightly and yet ever so loosely, as his skin fits him. . . . It hardens as his arteries harden. It is gaudy when he is young and gathers decorum when he grows old.
—H. L. MENCKEN, *Prejudices*, Fifth Series, IX, 5, 1926

The subjunctive mood is in its death throes, and the best thing to do is to put it out of its misery as soon as possible.
—W. SOMERSET MAUGHAM, *Writer's Notebook* (1949), 1941

The great enemy of clear language is insincerity. When there is a gap between one's real and one's declared aims, one turns as it were instinctively to long words and exhausted idioms, like a cuttle fish squirting out ink.

—GEORGE ORWELL, *Shooting an Elephant*, "Politics and the English Language," 1950

Political language – and with variations this is true of all political parties, from Conservatives to Anarchists – is designed to make lies sound truthful and murder respectable, and to give an appearance of solidity to pure wind.

—GEORGE ORWELL, *Shooting an Elephant*, "Politics and the English Language," 1950

Proletarian language is dictated by hunger. The poor chew words to fill their bellies. From the objective spirit of language they expect the sustenance refused them by society; those whose mouths are full of words have nothing else between their teeth. So they take revenge on language. Being forbidden to love it, they maim the body of language, and so repeat in impotent strength the disfigurement inflicted on them.

—THEODOR ADORNO, *Minima Moralia*, 65, 1951

Vague expression permits the hearer to imagine whatever suits him and what he already thinks in any case. Rigorous formulation demands unequivocal comprehension, conceptual effort, to which people are deliberately disencouraged, and imposes on them in advance of any content a suspension of all received opinions, and thus an isolation, that they violently resist.

—THEODOR ADORNO, *Minima Moralia*, 64, 1951

Criticism

The role of an author is rather presumptuous; it is that of one who believes himself in a position to give lessons to the public. And the role of the critic? He is even more presumptuous; it is that of one who believes himself in a position to give lessons to one who believes himself in a position to give lessons to the public.
—DENIS DIDEROT, *Discours sur la poésie dramatique*, 1758

I as a poet have a totally different interest from that of the critic. My business is to coordinate, to unite, to make a whole of differentiated parts; it is the critic's business to resolve, to analyze, to separate the most homogeneous whole into parts.
—JOHANN WOLFGANG VON GOETHE, conversation with Böttiger (Weigand transl.), spring, 1795

Reviewers, with some rare exceptions, are the most stupid and malignant race. As a bankrupt thief turns thief-taker in despair, so an unsuccessful author turns critic.
—PERCY BYSSHE SHELLEY, *Adonais*, "Preface" (suppressed by publisher), 1821

There is another mode [of criticism] which enters into the natural history of every thing that breathes and lives, which believes no impulse to be entirely in vain, which scrutinizes circumstances, motive, and object before it condemns, and believes there is a beauty in natural form, if its law and purpose be understood.
—MARGARET FULLER, "Poets of the People," in *Art, Literature and the Drama* (1860), 1840's

Criticism should not be querulous and wasting, all knife and root-puller, but guiding, instructive, inspiring, a south wind, not an east wind.
—RALPH WALDO EMERSON, *Journals*, June, 1847

You do not get a man's most effective criticism until you provoke him. Severe truth is expressed with some bitterness.
—HENRY DAVID THOREAU, *Journal*, March 15, 1854

Insects sting, not in malice, but because they want to live. It is the same with critics: they desire our blood, not our pain.
—FRIEDRICH NIETZSCHE, *Assorted Opinions and Maxims*, 164, 1879

The ability to accept criticism and contradiction is a sign of high culture. Some people actually realize that higher human beings desire and provoke contradiction in order to receive some hint about their own injustices of which they are as yet unaware.
—FRIEDRICH NIETZSCHE, *The Gay Science* (Kaufmann transl.), 297, 1882

When we criticize something, this is no arbitrary and impersonal event; it is, at least very often, evidence of vital energies in us that are growing and shedding a skin. We negate and must negate because something in us wants to live and affirm – something that we perhaps do not know or see as yet.
—FRIEDRICH NIETZSCHE, *The Gay Science* (Kaufmann transl.), 307, 1882

People have pointed out evidences of personal feeling in my notices as if they were accusing me of a misdemeanor, not knowing that a criticism written without personal feeling is not worth reading. . . . The true critic . . . is the man who becomes your personal enemy on the sole provocation of a bad performance, and will only be appeased by good performances.
—GEORGE BERNARD SHAW, *Music in London*, 1890-1894 (1930), September 3, 1890

It is only about things that do not interest one that one can give a really unbiased opinion, which is no doubt the reason why an unbiased opinion is always absolutely valueless. The man who sees both sides of a question is a man who sees absolutely nothing at all. . . . It is only an auctioneer who can equally and impartially admire all schools of Art.
—OSCAR WILDE, *Intentions*, "The Critic as Artist," 1891

There are two ways of disliking art. . . . One is to dislike it. The other, to like it rationally.
—OSCAR WILDE, *Intentions*, "The Critic as Artist," 1891

In this world if you do not say a thing in an irritating way, you may as well not say it at all, since nobody will trouble themselves about anything that does not trouble them. The attention given to a criticism is in direct proportion to its indigestibility.
—GEORGE BERNARD SHAW, *Our Theatres in the Nineties* (1930), April 4, 1896

Each generation of critics does nothing but take the opposite of the truths accepted by their predecessors.
—MARCEL PROUST, *Le côté de Guermantes*, 1921

The Arts

Never trust the artist. Trust the tale. The proper function of a critic is to save the tale from the artist who created it.
—D. H. LAWRENCE, *Studies in Classic American Literature*, 1, 1923

A critic must be able to *feel* the impact of a work of art in all its complexity and its force. To do so, he must be a man of force and complexity himself, which few critics are. A man with a paltry, impudent nature will never write anything but paltry, impudent criticism.
—D. H. LAWRENCE, "John Galsworthy," in D. H. Lawrence et. al., *Scrutinies*, 1928

It is the nature of the artist to mind excessively what is said about him. Literature is strewn with the wreckage of men who have minded beyond reason the opinions of others.
—VIRGINIA WOOLF, *A Room of One's Own*, 3, 1929

By reducing the work of art to its content and then interpreting *that*, one tames the work of art. Interpretation makes art manageable, conformable.
—SUSAN SONTAG, *Against Interpretation*, "Against Interpretation," 1966

Interpretation is the revenge of the intellect upon art.
—SUSAN SONTAG, *Against Interpretation*, "Against Interpretation," 1966

Human Affairs

Politics. Government

In a country that is well governed, consider it a dishonor to be poor and obscure; in a country that is badly governed, consider it a dishonor to be rich and famous.
—CONFUCIUS, *Analects*, VIII, 13, 6th-5th century B.C.

By art is created that great Leviathan, called a Commonwealth or State – in Latin *Civitas* – which is but an artificial man . . . and in which the sovereignty is an artificial soul.
—THOMAS HOBBES, *Leviathan*, "Introduction," 1651

The tyranny of a prince is no more damaging to a state than indifference towards the common good in a republic.
—CHARLES DE MONTESQUIEU, *Considérations sur les causes de la grandeur des Romains et de leur décadence*, 4, 1734

In a free nation it is often immaterial whether individuals reason well or badly; it is sufficient that they reason: from this comes the liberty which guarantees the consequences of these very same reasonings.
—CHARLES DE MONTESQUIEU, *The Spirit of the Laws*, XIX, 27, 1748

In general, the art of government consists in taking as much money as possible from one class of citizens and giving it to another.
—VOLTAIRE, *Philosophical Dictionary*, "Money," 1764

Government, like dress, is the badge of lost innocence; the palaces of kings are built upon the ruins of the bowers of paradise.
—THOMAS PAINE, *Common Sense*, "On the Origin and Design of Government in General," 1776

It would be a dangerous delusion were a confidence in the men of our choice to silence our fears for the safety of our rights: that confidence is everywhere the parent of despotism – free government is founded in jealousy, and not in confidence.
—THOMAS JEFFERSON, *Draft of the Kentucky Resolutions*, October, 1798

When a man assumes a public trust, he should consider himself as public property.
—THOMAS JEFFERSON, in a conversation with Baron Humboldt, 1807. Quoted in B.L. Rayner, *Life of Jefferson* (1832)

Despotism, or unlimited sovereignty, or absolute power, is the same in a majority of a popular assembly, an aristocratic council, an oligarchical junto, and a single emperor.
—JOHN ADAMS, letter to Thomas Jefferson, November 13, 1815

In politics as on the sickbed, people toss from one side to the other fancying that they will be more comfortable.
—JOHANN WOLFGANG VON GOETHE, conversation with von Müller (Weigand transl.), December 29, 1825

Government is emphatically a machine: to the discontented a "taxing machine," to the contented a "machine for securing property."
—THOMAS CARLYLE, *Critical and Miscellaneous Essays*, "Signs of the Times," 1838

The wise and just man will always feel that he stands on his own feet; that he imparts strength to the state, not receives security from it; and if all went down, he and such as he would quite easily combine in a new and better constitution.
—RALPH WALDO EMERSON, *Nature; Addresses, and Lectures*, "The Young American," 1849

Politics . . . are but the cigar-smoke of a man.
—HENRY DAVID THOREAU, "Walking," in *Excursions* (1863), 1862

I saw that the state was half-witted, that it was timid as a lone woman with her silver spoons, and that it did not know its friends from its foes, and I lost all my remaining respect for it, and pitied it.
—HENRY DAVID THOREAU, *Cape Cod*, 1865

Did you, too, O friend, suppose democracy was only for elections, for politics, and for a party name? I say democracy is only of use there that it may pass on and come to its flower and fruits in manners, in the highest forms of interaction between men, and their beliefs – in religion, literature, colleges, and schools – democracy in all public and private life, and in the army and navy.
—WALT WHITMAN, *Democratic Vistas*, 1871

For to democracy, the leveler, the unyielding principle of the average, is surely join'd another principle, equally unyielding, closely

tracking the first, indispensable to it, opposite. . . . This second principle is individuality, the pride and centripetal isolation of a human
being in himself – identity – personalism.
—WALT WHITMAN, *Democratic Vistas*, 1871

Political democracy, as it exists and practically works in America,
with all its threatening evils, supplies a training school for making
first-class men. It is life's gymnasium.
—WALT WHITMAN, *Democratic Vistas*, 1871

The society that will organize production on the basis of a free and
equal association of the producers will put the whole machinery of
state where it will then belong: into the museum of antiquities, by
the side of the spinning wheel and the bronze axe.
—FRIEDRICH ENGELS, *The Origin of the Family, Private Property, and
the State*, 1884

If in a democratic country nothing can be permanently achieved
save through the masses of the people, it will be impossible to establish a higher political life than the people themselves crave.
—JANE ADDAMS, *Twenty Years at Hull House*, 6, 1910

The State is the altar of political freedom and, like the religious altar,
it is maintained for the purpose of human sacrifice.
—EMMA GOLDMAN, *Anarchism and Other Essays*, "Anarchism: What it
Really Stands For," 1910

It is said that every people has the Government it deserves. It is more
to the point that every Government has the electorate it deserves; for

the orators of the front bench can edify or debauch an ignorant electorate at will.
—GEORGE BERNARD SHAW, *Heartbreak House*, "Preface," 1919

The Country, as an inescapable group into which we are born, and
which makes us its particular kind of a citizen of the world, seems
to be a fundamental fact of our consciousness. . . . But State is essentially a concept of power, of competition; it signifies a group in its
aggressive aspects. And we have the misfortune of being born not
only into a country but into a State, and as we grow up we learn to
mingle the two feelings into a hopeless confusion.
—RANDOLPH BOURNE, *Untimely Papers*, "The State," 1919

Only when the state is at war does the modern society function with
that unity of sentiment, simple uncritical patriotic devotion, coop-
eration of services, which have always been the ideal of the State
lover.
—RANDOLPH BOURNE, *Untimely Papers*, "The State," 1919

The whole aim of practical politics is to keep the populace alarmed
(and hence clamorous to be led to safety) by menacing it with an
endless series of hobgoblins, all of them imaginary.
—H. L. MENCKEN, *The Smart Set*, December, 1921

The ordinary man . . . is an Anarchist. He wants to do as he likes.
He may want his neighbor to be governed, but he himself doesn't
want to be governed.
—GEORGE BERNARD SHAW, *The Political Madhouse in America and
Nearer Home*, 1933

There is no antithesis between authoritarian government and democracy. All government is authoritarian; and the more democratic a government is the more authoritative it is; for with the people behind it, it can push its authority further than any Tsar or foreign despot dare do.

—GEORGE BERNARD SHAW, letter in *New Republic,* April 14, 1937

So Two cheers for Democracy: one because it admits variety and two because it permits criticism. Two cheers are quite enough: there is no occasion to give three.

—E. M. FORSTER, *Two Cheers for Democracy* (1951), "What I Believe," 1939

The worst government is the most moral. One composed of cynics is often very tolerant and humane. But when fanatics are on top there is no limit to oppression.

—H. L. MENCKEN, *Minority Report,* 327, 1956

Under democracy one party always devotes its chief energies to trying to prove that the other party is unfit to rule – and both commonly succeed, and are right.

—H. L. MENCKEN, *Minority Report,* 330, 1956

Two things are needed in a democracy: articulate and knowledgeable publics, and political leaders who if not men of reason are at least reasonably responsible to such knowledgeable publics as exist.

—C. WRIGHT MILLS, *The Power Elite,* 15, 1956

If I dream of a democratic Utopia, it will be one in which a parliamentary candidate can hope to attract votes by the boast that he discovered during the last year thirty-one mistakes made by himself and has managed to correct thirteen of them; while his competitor discovered only twenty-seven, even though he admittedly also corrected thirteen of them. I need not say that this will be a Utopia of toleration.

—KARL POPPER, "Toleration and Intellectual Responsibility," in S. Medus & D. Edwards, *On Toleration*, 1987

No Constitution, no Bill of Rights, no voting procedures, no piece of legislation can assure us peace or justice or equality. *That* requires a constant struggle, a continuous discussion among citizens, an endless series of organizations and movements, creating a pressure on whatever procedures there are.

—HOWARD ZINN, *Declarations of Independence: Cross-Examining American Ideology*, 9, 1990

Law. Justice

There is no such thing as justice in the abstract; it is merely a compact between men in their dealings with one another not to harm or be harmed.

—EPICURUS, *Practical Doctrines*, 33, 4th–3rd century B.C.

The laws derive their authority from possession and usage; it is dangerous to trace them back to their origin. They grow and gain in

dignity as they roll on, like our rivers: if one follows them upstream to their source, it is just a little trickle of water, hardly recognizable.
—MICHEL DE MONTAIGNE, *Essays*, II, 12, 1580

There is not a man so good that, were he to lay open to the scrutiny of the laws all his actions and thoughts, he would not deserve to be hanged ten times in his life. . . . And another man might be such as to never offend against the laws at all, who yet would not deserve to be commended as a man of virtue and whom philosophy would very justly order to be whipped.
—MICHEL DE MONTAIGNE, *Essays*, III, 9, 1588

Mere justice is, upon most occasions, but a negative virtue, and only hinders us from hurting our neighbour. The man who barely abstains from violating either the person or the estate, or the reputation, of his neighbors, has surely very little positive merit. He fulfills, however, all the rules of what is peculiarly called justice.
—ADAM SMITH, *The Theory of Moral Sentiments*, II, 2, 1, 1759

We should be men first, and subjects afterward. It is not desirable to cultivate a respect for the law, so much as for the right.
—HENRY DAVID THOREAU, "Civil Disobedience" in *A Yankee in Canada* (1866), 1849

They are the lovers of law and order who observe the law when the government breaks it.
—HENRY DAVID THOREAU, "Slavery in Massachusetts," lecture delivered in 1854

Find out just what any people will quietly submit to and you have found out the exact measure of injustice and wrong that will be imposed upon them, and these will continue till they are resisted with either words or blows or with both. The limits of tyrants are prescribed by the endurance of those whom they oppress.
—FREDERICK DOUGLASS, "West India Emancipation," speech delivered at Canandaigua, N.Y., August 4, 1857

Laws never would be improved if there were not numerous persons whose moral sentiments are better than the existing laws.
—JOHN STUART MILL, *The Subjection of Women*, 2, 1869

Distrust all in whom the impulse to punish is powerful. They are people of low stock and breeding; out of their countenances peer the hangman and the bloodhound. Distrust all those who talk much of their justice!
—FRIEDRICH NIETZSCHE, *Thus Spoke Zarathustra*, II, 7, 1883

The law is an adroit mixture of customs that are beneficial to society, and could be followed even if no law existed, and others that are of advantage to a ruling minority, but harmful to the masses of men, and can be enforced on them only by terror.
—PETER KROPOTKIN, *Words of a Rebel*, 1884

The law, in it majestic equality, forbids the rich as well as the poor to sleep under bridges, to beg in the streets, and to steal bread.
—ANATOLE FRANCE, *Le Lys rouge*, 7, 1894

The judicial nets are so adjusted as to catch the minnows and let the whales slip through, and the federal judge is as far removed from the common people as if he inhabited another planet.
—EUGENE V. DEBS, speech, November 23, 1895

The rulers make penal codes for the regulation and control of the earth and all the property thereon – the earth that was made long ages before they were evolved, and will still remain ages after they are dust. . . . They provide that it may pass from hand to hand forever.
— CLARENCE DARROW, *Resist Not Evil*, 1903

Between guilt and innocence there exists only the thickness of a sheet of paper with a stamp on it.
—ANATOLE FRANCE, *Crainquebille*, 1904

Injustice is relatively easy to bear; what stings is justice.
—H. L. MENCKEN, *Prejudices*, Third Series, III, 1922

My address is like my shoes. It travels with me. I abide where there is a fight against wrong.
—MOTHER JONES, quoted in Parton, *The Autobiography of Mother Jones*, 1925

If it had not been for this thing, I might have lived out my life talking at street corners to scorning men. . . . Never in our full life could we hope to do such work for tolerance, for justice, for man's understanding of man, as now we do by accident.
—BARTOLOMEO VANZETTI, letter to his son, April 9, 1927, shortly

before his execution for alleged robbery and murder (and implicitly for his anarchist beliefs). Historians have since exonerated him.

In a modern democratic community, justice means equality. But it would not mean equality in a community where there was a hierarchy of classes, recognized and accepted by inferiors as well as superiors. . . . I should therefore define justice as the arrangement producing the least envy.
—BERTRAND RUSSELL, *Sceptical Essays*, 13, 1928

The law is equal before all of us; but we are not all equal before the law. Virtually there is one law for the rich and another for the poor, one law for the cunning and another for the simple, one law for the forceful and another for the feeble, . . . and within family limits one law for the parent and no law at all for the child.
—GEORGE BERNARD SHAW, *The Millionairess*, "Preface," 1936

The denial that men may be arbitrary in human transactions is the higher law. . . . That is the spiritual essence without which the letter of the law is nothing but the formal trappings of vested rights or the ceremonial disguise of caprice and willfulness.
—WALTER LIPPMANN, *The Good Society*, XV, 5, 1937

Absolute justice is achieved by the suppression of all contradictions, therefore it destroys freedom.
—ALBERT CAMUS, *The Rebel*, "Historic Murder," 1951

It is a deception of the citizenry to claim that the "rule of law" has replaced the "rule of men." It is still men (women are mostly kept out of the process) who enact the laws, who sit on the bench and interpret them, who occupy the White House or the Governor's mansion and have the job of enforcing them.

—HOWARD ZINN, *Declarations of Independence: Cross-Examining American Ideology*, 6, 1990

Freedom

Men are mistaken in thinking themselves free; their opinion is made up of consciousness of their own actions and ignorance of the causes by which they are conditioned. Their idea of freedom, therefore, is simply their ignorance of any cause for their actions.

—BENEDICT DE SPINOZA, *Ethics*, II, Prop. 35, 1677

Freedom is like those solid and rich foods or those hearty wines, which are proper to nourish and fortify robust constitutions habituated to them, but which overpower, ruin, and intoxicate the weak and delicate who are unsuited for them. Once peoples are accustomed to masters, they are no longer able to do without them.

—JEAN-JACQUES ROUSSEAU, *Discourse on the Origin and Foundations of Inequality among Men* (Masters transl.), 1755

What we obtain too cheap, we esteem too lightly: 'Tis dearness only that gives every thing its value. Heaven knows how to set a proper price upon its goods: and it would be strange indeed, if so celestial an article as FREEDOM should not be highly rated.

—THOMAS PAINE, *The American Crisis*, No. 1, December 19, 1776

It is of great importance in a republic not only to guard the society against the oppression of its rulers, but to guard one part of the society against the injustice of the other part.
—JAMES MADISON, *The Federalist*, No. 51, 1788

Since the general civilization of mankind, I believe there are more instances of the abridgment of the freedom of the people by gradual and silent encroachments of those in power than by violent and sudden usurpations.
—JAMES MADISON, speech in the Virginia Convention, June 16, 1788

No one is more of a slave than he who thinks himself free without being so.
—JOHANN WOLFGANG VON GOETHE, *Maxims and Reflections*, 43, 1809

What is the good of a superabundance of freedom that we do not know how to use?
—JOHANN WOLFGANG VON GOETHE, *Conversations with Eckermann* (1836), January 18, 1827

The ideal republic is a positive anarchy. It is liberty free from all shackles, superstitions, prejudices, sophistries, usury, authority; it is reciprocal liberty and not limited liberty; liberty not the daughter but the Mother of order.
—PIERRE JOSEPH PROUDHON, *What is Property?* 1840

Those who profess to favor freedom, and yet depreciate agitation, are men who want rain without thunder and lightning. They want the ocean without the roar of its many waters.
—FREDERICK DOUGLASS, "West India Emancipation," speech delivered at Canandaigua, N.Y., August 4, 1857

Protection, therefore, against the tyranny of the magistrate is not enough: there needs protection also against the tyranny of the prevailing opinion and feeling; against the tendency of society to impose, by other means than civil penalties, its own ideas and practices as rules of conduct on those who dissent from them.
—JOHN STUART MILL, *On Liberty*, 1, 1859

The liberty of the individual must be thus far limited; he must not make himself a nuisance to other people.
—JOHN STUART MILL, *On Liberty*, 3, 1859

Nothing is more disgusting than the crowing about liberty by slaves, as most men are, and the flippant mistaking for freedom of some paper preamble like a Declaration of Independence, or the statute right to vote, by those who never dared to think or to act.
—RALPH WALDO EMERSON, *The Conduct of Life*, "Fate," 1860

With some the word liberty may mean for each man to do as he pleases with himself, and the product of his labor; while with others the same word may mean for some men to do as they please with other men, and the product of other men's labor. . . . And it follows that each of the things is, by the respective parties, called by two different and incompatible names – liberty and tyranny.
—ABRAHAM LINCOLN, speech delivered in Baltimore, April 18, 1864

A prohibition whose reason we do not understand or admit is not only for the obstinate man but also for the man thirsty for knowledge almost an injunction: let us put it to the test, so as to learn *why* this prohibition exists.
—FRIEDRICH NIETZSCHE, *The Wanderer and his Shadow* (Hollingdale transl.), 48, 1880

One of the qualities of liberty is that, as long as it is being striven after, it goes on expanding. Therefore, the man who stands still in the midst of the struggle and says, "I have it", merely shows by so doing that he has just lost it.
—HENRIK IBSEN, letter to Georg Brandes, January 3, 1882

My concept of freedom. The value of a thing sometimes does not lie in what one gains from it, but in what one pays for it – what it costs us.
—FRIEDRICH NIETZSCHE, *Twilight of the Idols*, "Skirmishes of an Untimely Man," 38, 1889

Freedom in this field [the sphere of material production] can only consist in socialized man, the associated producers, rationally regulating their interchange with Nature, bringing it under their common control, instead of their being ruled by it as by the blind forces of Nature.
—KARL MARX, *Capital*, Vol. III, 1894

It is by the goodness of God that in our country we have those unspeakably precious things: freedom of speech, freedom of conscience, and the prudence never to practice either of them.
—MARK TWAIN, *Following the Equator*, Vol. I, 20, "Pudd'nhead Wilson's New Calendar," 1897

The love of liberty, which sharpens itself on the millstone of monarchy and absolutism, becomes dulled in a country which is free or considers itself to be free.
—ANATOLE FRANCE, *Monsieur Bergeret à Paris*, 9, 1901

Liberty means responsibility. That is why most men dread it.
—GEORGE BERNARD SHAW, *Man and Superman*, "Maxims for Revolutionists," 1903

Liberty trains for liberty. Responsibility is the first step in responsibility.
—W. E. B. DUBOIS, *John Brown, A Biography*, "The Legacy of John Brown," 1909

Liberty is the breath of life to nations; and liberty is the one thing that parents, schoolmasters, and rulers spend their lives in extirpating for the sake of an immediately quiet and finally disastrous life.
—GEORGE BERNARD SHAW, *Misalliance*, "Preface," 1914

Freedom only for the supporters of the government, only for the members of one party – no matter how big its membership may be – is no freedom at all. Freedom is always and exclusively for the one who thinks differently.
—ROSA LUXEMBURG, *The Russian Revolution*, ca. 1918

There is a personal discipline necessary to the use of liberty. Without the discipline men never will love liberty and never will cherish it. They will be like a savage who by accident finds a delicate instrument and carelessly throws it away.
—WALTER LIPPMANN, "The South and the New Society," in Rossiter & Lare, eds., *The Essential Lippmann* (1963), 1927

It is clear that thought is not free if the profession of certain opinions makes it impossible to earn a living.
—BERTRAND RUSSELL, *Sceptical Essays*, 12, 1928

Democracy is so often and so naturally associated in our minds with freedom of *action*, forgetting the importance of freed intelligence which is necessary to direct and to warrant freedom of action. . . . The basic freedom is that of freedom of *mind*.
—JOHN DEWEY, "Democracy and Educational Administration," reprinted in Ratner, ed., *Intelligence in the Modern World* (1939), 1937

Acting against the command of authority, committing a sin, is in its positive human aspect the first act of freedom, that is, the first *human* act. In the myth the sin in its formal aspect is the acting against God's command; in its material aspect it is the eating of the tree of knowledge. The act of disobedience as an act of freedom is the beginning of reason.
—ERICH FROMM, *Escape from Freedom*, 2, 1941

"Freedom from" is not identical with positive freedom, with "freedom to."
—ERICH FROMM, *Escape from Freedom*, 2, 1941

Smokers and non-smokers cannot be equally free in the same railway carriage.
—GEORGE BERNARD SHAW, *Everybody's Political What's What?* 1944

A free society cannot be the substitution of a "new order" for the old order; it is the extension of spheres of free action until they make up most of the social life.
—PAUL GOODMAN, *The May Pamphlet*, "Reflections on Drawing the Line," 1945

Man is condemned to be free. Condemned, because he did not create himself, yet in other respects is free; because, once thrown into the world, he is responsible for everything he does.

—JEAN-PAUL SARTRE, *Existentialism is a Humanism*, "The Humanism of Existentialism," 1947

Liberty is one of the conscious values of a civilization. It is conceived and cultivated, defined and protected: it can also be abrogated, denied, perverted. But freedom is the *unconscious* creation of a culture. . . . It is a pulse, a living breath of which we are scarcely aware until it ceases.

—HERBERT READ, *Existentialism, Marxism, and Anarchism*, "Chains of Freedom," 1949

Freedom to criticize is held to compensate for the freedom to err – this is the American system. . . . One is assured, gently, that one has the freedom to criticize, as though this freedom, *in itself*, as it attaches to a single individual, counterbalanced the unjust law on the books.

—MARY McCARTHY, *On the Contrary* (1961), "No News, or What Killed the Dog," 1952

Liberty is liberty, not equality or fairness or justice or culture, or human happiness or a quiet conscience.

—ISAIAH BERLIN, *Two Concepts of Liberty*, 1, 1958

Men *are* free – as distinguished from their possessing the gift of freedom – as long as they act, neither before nor after; for to *be* free and to act are the same.

—HANNAH ARENDT, *Between Past and Future*, "What is Freedom," 1961

We can hardly rest comfortably with the assumption that freedom declines as equality . . . increases. It may be true that equality is inversely related to the freedom to dispose of and make use of property under the social arrangements of capitalism, but the latter condition is not to be simply identified as "freedom."
—NOAM CHOMSKY, "Equality," in W. Feinberg, *Equality and Social Policy*, 1978

I call upon the intellectual community in this country and abroad to stand up for freedom of the imagination, an issue much larger than my book or indeed my life.
—SALMAN RUSHDIE, press statement, February 14, 1989

Reform. Progress

Laws and institutions must go hand in hand with the progress of the human mind. As that becomes more developed, more enlightened, as new discoveries are made, new truths disclosed, . . . institutions must advance also, and keep pace with the times. We might as well require a man to wear still the coat that fitted him when a boy, as civilized society to remain ever under the regimen of their barbarous ancestors.
—THOMAS JEFFERSON, letter to Samuel Kercheval, July 12, 1816

Men are conservatives when they are least vigorous, or when they are most luxurious. They are conservatives after dinner, or before taking their rest; when they are sick or aged. In the morning, or when their

intellect or conscience has been aroused, when they hear music, or when they read poetry, they are radicals.
—RALPH WALDO EMERSON, *Essays*, Second Series, "New England Reformers," 1844

I know that compromises are often inevitable in practice, but I think they should be left to the enemy to propose – reformers should assert principles and only *accept* compromises.
—JOHN STUART MILL, letter to William J. Fox, late 1849

The whole history of the progress of human liberty shows that all concessions yet made to her august claims have been born of earnest struggle. . . . If there is no struggle there is no progress.
—FREDERICK DOUGLASS, "West India Emancipation," speech delivered at Canandaigua, N.Y., August 4, 1857

How fortunate it is for us all that it is somewhat unnatural for a human being to obey. Universal obedience is universal stagnation; disobedience is one of the conditions of progress.
—ROBERT G. INGERSOLL, *Individuality*, 1873

A small and temporary improvement may really be the worst enemy of a great and permanent improvement, unless the first is made on the lines and in the direction of the second. . . . The small reform may become the enemy of the great one.
—JOHN MORLEY, *On Compromise*, 3, 1874

England will never be civilised till she has added Utopia to her dominions.
—OSCAR WILDE, *Intentions*, "The Critic as Artist," 1891

The plain working truth is that it is not only good for people to be shocked occasionally, but absolutely necessary to the progress of society that they should be shocked pretty often.
—GEORGE BERNARD SHAW, *The Quintessence of Ibsenism*, "The Lesson of the Plays," 1891

The radical of one century is the conservative of the next. The radical invents the views. When he has worn them out the conservative adopts them.
—MARK TWAIN, *Mark Twain's Notebook* (1935), summer, 1898

All progress is based upon a universal, innate desire on the part of every organism to live beyond its income.
—SAMUEL BUTLER, *Note-Books* (1912), 1, late 19th century

The reasonable man adapts himself to the world: the unreasonable one persists in trying to adapt the world to himself. Therefore all progress depends on the unreasonable man.
—GEORGE BERNARD SHAW, *Man and Superman*, "Maxims for Revolutionists," 1903

Conservative, n. A statesman who is enamoured of existing evils, as distinguished from the liberal, who wishes to replace them with others.
—AMBROSE BIERCE, *The Devil's Dictionary*, 1906

All philanthropy – no age has seen more of it than our own – is only a savoury fumigation burning at the mouth of a sewer. This incense offering makes the air more endurable to passersby, but it does not hinder the infection in the sewer from spreading.
—ELLEN KEY, *The Century of the Child*, 1909

The strength and beauty of the radical's position is that he already to a large extent lives in that sort of world which he desires. . . . He sees the "muddle" around him, but what he actually feels and lives are the germs of the future.
—RANDOLPH BOURNE, *Youth and Life*, "For Radicals," 1913

You have to make more noise than anybody else, you have to make yourself more obtrusive than anybody else, you have to fill all the papers more than anybody else, in fact you have to be there all the time and see that they do not snow you under, if you are really going to get your reform realized.
—EMMELINE PANKHURST, "When Civil War is Waged by Women," speech delivered November 13, 1913. Quoted in Pankhurst, *My Own Story* (1914)

Restlessness is discontent – and discontent is the first necessity of progress. Show me a thoroughly satisfied man and I will show you a failure.
—THOMAS A. EDISON, *The Diary and Sundry Observations* (1948), early 20th century

The truth is that things change much faster and more dangerously when they are let alone than when they are carefully looked after.
—GEORGE BERNARD SHAW, *The Intelligent Woman's Guide to Socialism*, 13, 1928

The libertarian is rather a millenarian than a utopian. He does not look forward to a future state of things which he tries to bring about by suspect means. . . . *Merely by continuing to exist and act in nature*

and freedom, the libertarian wins the victory, establishes the society; it is not necessary for him to be the victor *over* anyone.
—PAUL GOODMAN, *The May Pamphlet*, "Reflections on Drawing the Line," 1945

Whatever there be of progress in life comes not through adaptation but through daring, through obeying the blind urge.
—HENRY MILLER, *The Wisdom of the Heart*, "Reflections on Writing," 1947

One must choose between God and Man, and all "radicals" and "progressives," from the mildest Liberals to the most extreme Anarchists, have in effect chosen Man.
—GEORGE ORWELL, *Shooting an Elephant*, "Reflections on Gandhi," 1950

The true criterion of reform is not its tempo but its realism, its true "radicalism"; it is the question whether it goes to the roots and attempts to change causes – or whether it remains on the surface and attempts to deal only with symptoms.
—ERICH FROMM, *The Sane Society*, VIII, 1955

Revolution

What country can preserve its liberties if their rulers are not warned from time to time that their people preserve the spirit of resistance? Let them take arms. . . . The tree of liberty must be refreshed from

time to time, with the blood of patriots and tyrants. It is its natural manure.
—THOMAS JEFFERSON, letter to William S. Smith, November 13, 1787

Law-givers or revolutionaries who promise both equality and freedom at one and the same time are either dreamers or charlatans.
—JOHANN WOLFGANG VON GOETHE, *Maxims and Reflections* (Stopp transl.), 953, 1833

But simply because we are at the head of a new movement, let us not set ourselves up as the leaders of a new intolerance, let us not pose as the apostles of a new religion – even though this religion be the religion of logic, the religion of reason itself . . . Let us never regard a question as closed, and even after we have exhausted our last argument, let us begin again, if necessary with eloquence and irony.
—PIERRE JOSEPH PROUDHON, letter to Karl Marx, May 17, 1846

All men recognize the right of revolution: that is, the right to refuse allegiance to, and to resist, the government when its tyranny or its inefficiency are great and unendurable.
—HENRY DAVID THOREAU, "Civil Disobedience," in *A Yankee in Canada* (1866), 1849

No social order ever perishes before all the productive forces for which there is room in it have developed; and new, higher relations of production never appear before the material conditions of their existence have matured in the womb of the old society itself.
—KARL MARX, *A Contribution to the Critique of Political Economy*, "Preface," 1859

Historically, the errors committed by a truly revolutionary movement are infinitely more fruitful than the infallibility of the cleverest Central Committee.
—ROSA LUXEMBURG, "Leninism or Marxism?" 2, 1904

Here I am . . . by class a respectable man, by common sense a hater of waste and disorder . . . and by temperament apprehensive and economically disposed to the limit of old-maidishness; yet I am, and have always been, and shall now always be, a revolutionary writer, because our laws make law impossible; our liberties destroy all freedom; our property is organized robbery; our morality is an impudent hypocrisy.
—GEORGE BERNARD SHAW, *Major Barbara*, "Preface," 1907

The ultimate end of all revolutionary social change is to establish the sanctity of human life, the dignity of man, the right of every human being to liberty and well-being.
—EMMA GOLDMAN, *My Further Disillusionment in Russia*, 1924

No revolution ever succeeds as a factor of liberation unless the means used to further it be identified in spirit and tendency with the purpose to be achieved.
—EMMA GOLDMAN, *My Further Disillusionment in Russia*, 1924

A revolution is not a dinner party, or writing an essay, or painting a picture, or doing embroidery; it cannot be so refined, so leisurely and gentle, so temperate, kind, courteous, restrained and magnanimous. A revolution is an insurrection, an act of violence by which one class overthrows another.
—MAO TSE-TUNG, *Report on an Investigation of the Peasant Movement in Hunan*, 1927

The insurrection, which rises above a revolution like a peak in the mountain chain of its events, can no more be evoked at will than the revolution as a whole. The masses advance and retreat several times before they make up their minds to the final assault.
—LEON TROTSKY, *History of the Russian Revolution*, Part III, 6, 1931–33

The Revolutionary wants to change the world; he transcends it and moves toward the future, towards an order of values which he himself invents. The rebel is careful to preserve the abuses from which he suffers so that he can go on rebelling against them.
—JEAN-PAUL SARTRE, *Baudelaire*, 1947

The revolution, first of all, proposes to satisfy the spirit of rebellion which has given rise to it; then it is compelled to deny it, the better to affirm itself. There is, it would seem, an ineradicable opposition between the movement of rebellion and the attainments of revolution.
—ALBERT CAMUS, *The Rebel*, "Thought at the Meridian," 1951

Every revolutionary ends by becoming either an oppressor or a heretic.
—ALBERT CAMUS, *The Rebel*, "Historical Rebellion" 1951

I believe in the armed struggle as the only solution for those people who fight to free themselves, and I am consistent with my beliefs. Many will call me an adventurer – and that I am, only one of a different sort: one of those who risks his skin to prove his platitudes.
—CHE GUEVARA, last letter to his parents before leaving to join guerillas in Bolivian jungle, 1965

Just as one could speak of the *fanshen* of the individual and the *fanshen* of the community, one could also speak of the *fanshen* of the nation, that process by which a whole people "turned over," that process by which a whole continent stood up.
—WILLIAM HINTON, *Fanshen: A Documentary of Revolution in a Chinese Village*, 67, 1966

Change never occurred across the board at the same rate. No social aggregation could advance as a block. Its individual members possessed varying degrees of awareness and varying capacities for learning and growth. In real life one had to depend on the more advanced to lead the less advanced and on the less advanced to lead the backward.
—WILLIAM HINTON, *Fanshen: A Documentary of Revolution in a Chinese Village*, 67, 1966

This, then, is the great humanistic and historical task of the oppressed: to liberate themselves and their oppressors as well.
—PAULO FREIRE, *Pedagogy of the Oppressed*, 1, 1970

War

Although fraud is detestable in all other activities, yet in the conduct of war it is laudable and honorable; and one who vanquishes an enemy by deceit is as much to be praised as one who does so by force.
—NICCOLO MACHIAVELLI, *Discourses*, III, 40, 1531

Every one may begin a war at his pleasure, but cannot so easily finish it.
—NICCOLO MACHIAVELLI, *Discourses*, II, 10, 1531

In my opinion, *there never was a good War, or a bad Peace*. What vast additions to the Conveniences and Comforts of Living might Mankind have acquired, if the Money spent in Wars had been employed in Works of Public utility!
—BENJAMIN FRANKLIN, letter to Sir Joseph Banks, July 27, 1783

Each government accuses the other of perfidy, intrigue, and ambition, as a means of heating the imagination of their respective nations, and incensing them to hostilities. Man is not the enemy of man, but through the medium of a false system of government.
—THOMAS PAINE, *The Rights of Man*, I, 1791

One lived always between the forces of order and the forces of disorder, between efforts to restrain and efforts to destroy, between payment and plunder, and this is what makes war so corrupting for the spirit. At one moment you play the role of bold destroyer, at another that of gentle restorer of life.
—JOHANN WOLFGANG VON GOETHE, *Campaign in France*, September 3, 1792

As long as war is regarded as wicked, it will always have its fascination. When it is looked upon as vulgar, it will cease to be popular.
—OSCAR WILDE, *Intentions*, "The Critic as Artist," 1891

Soldiering, my dear madam, is the coward's art of attacking mercilessly when you are strong, and keeping out of harm's way when you

are weak. That is the whole secret of successful fighting. Get your enemy at a disadvantage; and never, on any account, fight him on equal terms.
—GEORGE BERNARD SHAW, Sergius in *Arms and the Man*, II, 1894

One hears of the mechanical equivalent of heat. What we now need to discover in the social realm is the moral equivalent of war: something heroic that will speak to men as universally as war does, and yet will be as compatible with their spiritual selves as war has proved itself to be incompatible.
—WILLIAM JAMES, *The Varieties of Religious Experience*, 14 & 15, 1902

To fight is a radical instinct. . . . To fight for a reason and in a calculating spirit is something your true warrior despises.
—GEORGE SANTAYANA, *Reason in Society*, 3, 1905

You cannot build up a standing army and then throw it back into a box like tin soldiers. Armies equipped to the teeth with weapons . . . have their own dynamic functions.
—EMMA GOLDMAN, "Preparedness: The Road to Universal Slaughter," *Mother Earth*, 1915

The worst barbarity of war is that it forces men collectively to commit acts against which individually they would revolt with their whole being.
—ELLEN KEY, *War, Peace, and the Future*, 1916

O Lord our Father, our young patriots, idols of our hearts, go forth to battle – be thou near them! . . . O Lord our God, help us to tear their soldiers to bloody shreds with our shells; help us to cover their smiling fields with the pale forms of their patriot dead; help us to drown the thunder of the guns with the shrieks of their wounded. . . . We ask it in the spirit of love, of Him who is the Source of Love, and who is the ever-faithful refuge and friend of all who are sore beset and seek His aid with humble and contrite hearts. Amen.

—MARK TWAIN, quoted posthumously in *Harper's Magazine*, November, 1916

In the freest of republics as well as in the most tyrannical of empires, all foreign policy, the diplomatic negotiations which produce or forestall war, are equally the private property of the Executive part of the Government, and are equally exposed to no check whatever from popular bodies. . . . The moment war is declared, however, the mass of the people, through some spiritual alchemy, become convinced that they have willed and executed the deed themselves.

—RANDOLPH BOURNE, *Untimely Papers*, "The State," 1919

Wartime brings the ideal of the State out into very clear relief, and reveals attitudes and tendencies that were hidden. . . . For war is essentially the health of the State.

—RANDOLPH BOURNE, *Untimely Papers*, "The State," 1919

If wars are ever done away with, their cessation will not be due to sentimental arguments, but to the fact that science and invention may make war so dangerous to everyone concerned that the sheer patriotism of educated people in all nations . . . will be universally against the stupid war idea.

—THOMAS A. EDISON, *The Diary and Sundry Observations* (1948), 1927

I had seen nothing sacred, and the things that were glorious had no glory and the sacrifices were like the stockyards of Chicago if nothing was done with the meat except to bury it.
—ERNEST HEMINGWAY, *Farewell to Arms*, 27, 1929

You cannot divide my conscience into a war department and a peace department. Do you suppose that a man who will commit murder for political ends will hesitate to commit theft for personal ends? Do you suppose that you can make a man the mortal enemy of sixty million of his fellow creatures without making him a little less scrupulous about his next door neighbor?
—GEORGE BERNARD SHAW, Aubrey in *Too True to be Good*, III, 1932

What they could use around here is a good war. What else can you expect with peace running wild all over the place? You know what the trouble with peace is? No organization.
—BERTOLT BRECHT, Sergeant in *Mother Courage*, I, 1939

It would repel me less to be a hangman than a soldier, because the one is obliged to put to death only criminals sentenced by the law, but the other kills honest men who like himself bathe in innocent blood at the bidding of some superior.
—GEORGE SANTAYANA, *Persons and Places*, Vol. I, 2, 1944. Quoting the words of his mother

I am a *dedicated* but not an *absolute* pacifist; this means that I am opposed to the use of force under any circumstances except when confronted by an enemy who pursues the destruction of life as an *end in itself*.
—ALBERT EINSTEIN, letter to a Japanese correspondent, June 23, 1953. Quoted in Calaprice, *The Quotable Einstein* (1996)

Great Freethinkers

War will never cease until babies begin to come into the world with larger cerebrums and smaller adrenal glands.
—H. L. MENCKEN, *Minority Report*, 164, 1956

The French Revolution introduced a new kind of war, one in which the whole nation participated enthusiastically because it believed that it had something of value to defend. . . . From that time until the present day, governments have increasingly realized the necessity of making wars popular, and have used the potent weapon of popular education to that end.
—BERTRAND RUSSELL, *Understanding History*, "How to Read and Understand History," 1957

I'd like to see the government get out of war altogether and leave the whole field to private industry.
—JOSEPH HELLER, *Catch-22*, 24, 1961

The thugs honestly believe it their duty to commit murders, but the government does not acquiesce. The conscientious objectors honestly hold the opposite opinion, and again the government does not acquiesce. Killing is a state prerogative; it is equally criminal to do it unbidden and not to do it when bidden.
—BERTRAND RUSSELL, *Political Ideals*, 4, 1963

The insight that peace is the end of war, and that therefore a war is the preparation for peace, is at least as old as Aristotle, and the pretense that the aim of an armament race is to guard the peace is even older.
—HANNAH ARENDT, *On Revolution*, 1963

What war has always been is a puberty ceremony. It's a very rough one, but you went away a boy and came back a man, maybe with an eye missing or whatever but godammit you were a man and people had to call you a man thereafter.
—KURT VONNEGUT, interview in *City Limits*, March 11, 1983

What is it about our species that has made us see in war a kind of sacrament? . . . Which are we: beasts because we make war, or angels because we so often seek to make it into something holy?
—BARBARA EHRENREICH, *Blood Rites: Origins and History of the Passions of War*, 1, 1997

Nationalism. Patriotism

Not because Socrates said it, but because it is my true feeling, and perhaps to some excess, I regard all men as my compatriots, and embrace a Pole as I do a Frenchman, subordinating this national tie to the universal and common one.
—MICHEL DE MONTAIGNE, *Essays*, III, 9, 1588

The love of our own country seems not to be derived from the love of mankind. The former sentiment is altogether independent of the latter, and seems sometimes even to dispose us to act inconsistently with it.
—ADAM SMITH, *The Theory of Moral Sentiments*, VI, 2, 2, 1759

It is lamentable that to be a good patriot we must become the enemy of the rest of mankind.
—VOLTAIRE, *The Philosophical Dictionary*, "Country," 1764

I confess I am a little cynical on some topics, and when a whole nation is roaring Patriotism at the top of its voice, I am fain to explore the cleanness of its hands and purity of its heart.
—RALPH WALDO EMERSON, *Journals*, December 10, 1824

It is true that every foot of soil has its proper quality, that the grape on either side of the same fence has its own flavor, and so every acre on the globe, every group of people, every point of climate has its own moral meaning whereof it is the symbol. For such a patriotism let us stand.
—RALPH WALDO EMERSON, *Journals*, September-October, 1847

The strongest bond of human sympathy outside the family relation should be one uniting all working people of all nations and tongues, and kindreds.
—ABRAHAM LINCOLN, reply to New York Workingmen's Association, March 21, 1864

Patriotism is nationally that which egoism is individually – has, in fact, the same root; and along with kindred benefits brings kindred evils. Estimation of one's society is a reflex of self-estimation; and assertion of one's society's claims is an indirect assertion of one's own claims as a part of it.
—HERBERT SPENCER, *The Study of Sociology*, IX, 1873

Patriotism is a kind of religion; it is the egg from which wars are hatched.
—GUY DE MAUPASSANT, "My Uncle Sosthenes," in *Gil Blas*, August 12, 1882

He loves his country best who strives to make it best.
—ROBERT G. INGERSOLL, "Decoration Day Address," delivered in New York, May 29, 1882

Patriotism is, fundamentally, a conviction that a particular country is the best in the world because you were born in it.
—GEORGE BERNARD SHAW, *Music in London, 1890-1894* (1930), November 15, 1893

It would therefore seem obvious that patriotism as a feeling is a bad and harmful feeling and as a doctrine is a stupid doctrine. For it is clear that if each people and each State considers itself the best of peoples and States, they all dwell in a gross and harmful delusion.
—LEO TOLSTOY, "Patriotism and Government," 1, 1900

A healthy nation is as unconscious of its nationality as a healthy man of his bones. But if you break a nation's nationality it will think of nothing else but getting it set again.
—GEORGE BERNARD SHAW, *John Bull's Other Island*, "Preface," 1907

The flag is not a symbol of the country as a cultural group, following certain ideals of life, but solely a symbol of the political State, inseparable from its prestige and expansion.
—RANDOLPH BOURNE, *Untimely Papers*, "The State," 1919

Nationalism is an infantile disease. It is the measles of mankind.
—ALBERT EINSTEIN, statement to G. S. Viereck. Recorded in Dukas & Hoffmann, eds., *Albert Einstein: The Human Side* (1979), 1921

If my theory of relativity is proven successful, Germany will claim me as a German and France will declare that I am a citizen of the world. Should my theory prove untrue, France will say that I am a German, and Germany will declare that I am a Jew.
—ALBERT EINSTEIN, from an address to the French Philosophical Society at the Sorbonne, April 6, 1922. Quoted in Calaprice, *The Quotable Einstein* (1996)

Patriotism, as I see it, is often an arbitary veneration of real estate above principles.
—GEORGE JEAN NATHAN, statement in Einstein et. al., *Living Philosophies*, 1931

Andrea: Unhappy the country that has no heroes! Galileo: No. Unhappy the country that needs heroes.
—BERTOLT BRECHT, *Life of Galileo*, XII, 1939

Just as love for one individual which excludes the love for others is not love, love for one's country which is not part of one's love for humanity is not love, but idolatrous worship.
—ERICH FROMM, *The Sane Society*, III, 1955

There's a great deal to be said for nationalism, for keeping diversity – in literature, in art, in language, and in all kinds of cultural things. But when it comes to politics, I think nationalism is unmitigated evil.
—BERTRAND RUSSELL, *Bertrand Russell Speaks his Mind*, 8, 1960

No matter that patriotism is too often the refuge of scoundrels. Dissent, rebellion, and all-around hell-raising remain the true duty of patriots.
—BARBARA EHRENREICH, *The Worst Years of our Lives*, "Introduction," 1990

Society

He who is unable to live in society, or who has no need because he is sufficient for himself, must be either a beast or a god.
—ARISTOTLE, *Politics*, I, 2, 4th Century B.C.

Not the good and amiable, but the bad and hateful qualities of man, his imperfections and the want of excellencies which other creatures are endowed with, are the first causes that made man sociable beyond other animals, the moment after he lost Paradise.
—BERNARD MANDEVILLE, *Fable of the Bees*, "A Search into the Nature of Society," 1723

It is as impossible for a society to take shape and survive without self-love [among its members] as it would be for a person to produce children without sexual desire or to think of nourishing himself without appetite, etc. It is love of ourselves which supports love of others; it is through our mutual needs that we are useful to mankind.
—VOLTAIRE, *Philosophical Letters*, 25, "On the Thoughts of Pascal," 1734

The first person who, having enclosed a piece of ground, took it into his head to say "This is mine," and found people simple enough to believe him, was the real founder of civil society. How many crimes, wars, murders, and how many horrors and misfortunes would mankind have been spared by someone who, uprooting the stakes or filling in the ditch, had shouted to his fellow men: "Beware of listening to this imposter; you are lost if you once forget that the fruits of the earth belong to us all and the earth itself to no one!"
—JEAN-JACQUES ROUSSEAU, *Discourse on the Origin and Foundations of Inequality among Men*, 1755

The moment you enter society, you draw the key from your heart and put it in your pocket. Those who fail to do so are fools.
—JOHANN WOLFGANG VON GOETHE, conversation with Lavater (Weigand transl.), June 26, 1774

Society is produced by our wants, and government by our wickedness; the former promotes our happiness *positively* by uniting our affections, the latter *negatively* by restraining our vices.
—THOMAS PAINE, *Common Sense*, "On the Origin and Design of Government in General," 1776

The more equality there is established among men, the more virtue and happiness will reign in society.
—MARY WOLLSTONECRAFT, *A Vindication of the Rights of Woman*, 1, 1792

Society is a joint-stock company, in which the members agree, for better securing of his bread to each shareholder, to surrender the liberty and culture of the eater.
—RALPH WALDO EMERSON, *Essays*, First Series, "Self-Reliance," 1841

Human Affairs

A number of porcupines huddled together for warmth on a cold day in winter; but, as they began to prick one another with their quills, they were obliged to disperse. . . . At last, after many turns of huddling and dispersing, they discovered that they would be best off by remaining at a little distance from one another. In the same way the need of society drives the human porcupines together, only to be mutually repelled by the many prickly and disagreeable qualities of their nature. The moderate distance which they at last discover to be the only tolerable condition of intercourse is the code of politeness and fine manners.

—ARTHUR SCHOPENHAUER, *Parerga and Paralipomena*, Vol. II, 31, 1851

Man is in the most literal sense of the word a *zoon politikon*, not merely a social animal, but an animal which can develop into an individual only in society.

—KARL MARX, *Foundations of the Critique of Political Economy*, 1857-58

The security of society lies in custom and unconscious instinct, and the basis of the stability of society, as a healthy organism, is the complete absence of any intelligence among its members.

—OSCAR WILDE, *Intentions*, "The Critic as Artist," 1891

The relations between the individual and society are like a roulette table. Society is the banker. Individuals sometimes win and sometimes lose; but the banker wins always.

—W. SOMERSET MAUGHAM, *A Writer's Notebook* (1949), 1894

We maintain that under *any* circumstances sociability is the greatest advantage in the struggle for life. Those species which willingly or unwillingly abandon it are doomed to decay.
—PETER KROPOTKIN, *Mutual Aid*, 1902

Where public spirit has held best, as at Sparta or . . . among the Jesuits, it has been paid for by a notable lack of spontaneity and wisdom; such inhuman devotion to an arbitrary end has made these societies odious. We may say, therefore, that a zeal sufficient to destroy selfishness is, as men are now constituted, worse than selfishness itself.
—GEORGE SANTAYANA, *Reason in Society*, 5, 1905

There are very many more hypocrites than truly civilized persons – indeed, it is a debatable point whether a certain degree of hypocrisy be not indispensable for the maintenance of civilization.
—SIGMUND FREUD, "Thoughts for the Times on War and Death," *Imago*, 5, 1915

We all deprecate prejudice; but if all of us were not animated sacks of prejudices, and at least nine tenths of them were not the same prejudices so deeply rooted that we never think of them as prejudices but call them common sense, we could no more form a community than so many snakes.
—GEORGE BERNARD SHAW, *The Intelligent Woman's Guide to Socialism and Capitalism*, 81, 1928

It is always possible to bind together a considerable number of people in love, so long as there are other people left over to receive the manifestations of their aggressiveness.
—SIGMUND FREUD, *Civilization and Its Discontents*, 5, 1930

The public and the private worlds are inseparably connected . . . the tyrannies and servilities of the one are the tyrannies and servilities of the other.
—VIRGINIA WOOLF, *Three Guineas*, 1938

The fundamentally social nature of all living things has its origin in this physiological relationship between parent and offspring; in the fact that the two are for a time bound together in an interactive association.
—ASHLEY MONTAGU, *On Being Human*, "What is the Nature of Life?" 1950

Evolution itself is a process which favors co-operating rather than disoperating groups, and "fitness" is a function of the group as a whole rather than of separate individuals.
—ASHLEY MONTAGU, *On Being Human*, "What is the Nature of Life?" 1950

Our social scientists have become so accustomed to the highly organized and by-and-large smoothly running society that they have begun to think that "social animal" means "harmoniously belonging." They do not like to think that fighting and dissenting are proper social functions, nor that rebelling or initiating fundamental change is a social function.
—PAUL GOODMAN, *Growing Up Absurd*, "Introduction," 1960

In this book I shall therefore take the opposite tack and ask, "Socialization to what? to what dominant society and available culture?"
—PAUL GOODMAN, *Growing Up Absurd*, "Introduction," 1960

Economy

Pride, sloth, sensuality, and fickleness are the great patrons that promote all arts and sciences, trades, handicrafts, and callings.
—BERNARD MANDEVILLE, *Fable of the Bees*, "A Search into the Nature of Society," 1723

Every individual necessarily labours to render the annual revenue of the society as great as he can. He generally, indeed, neither intends to promote the public interest, nor knows how much he is promoting it. . . . He intends only his own gain, and he is in this, as in many other cases, led by an invisible hand to promote an end which was no part of his intention.
—ADAM SMITH, *Wealth of Nations*, IV, 2, 1776

People of the same trade seldom meet together, even for merriment and diversion, but their conversation ends in a conspiracy against the public, or in some contrivance to raise prices.
—ADAM SMITH, *Wealth of Nations*, I, 10, 2, 1776

No society can surely be flourishing and happy, of which the far greater part are poor and miserable. It is but equity, besides, that they who feed, clothe, and lodge the whole body of the people, should have such a share of the produce of their own labour as to be themselves tolerably well fed, clothed, and lodged.
—ADAM SMITH, *Wealth of Nations*, I, 8, 1776

The worker becomes all the poorer the more wealth he produces, the more his production increases in power and range. . . . The devaluation of the world of men proceeds in direct proportion with the increasing value of the world of things.
—KARL MARX, *Economic and Philosophic Manuscripts*, 1844

Labor is prior to and independent of capital. Capital is only the fruit of labor, and could never have existed if labor had not first existed. Labor is the superior of capital, and man deserves much the higher consideration.
—ABRAHAM LINCOLN, *First Annual Message to Congress*, Regular Session, December 3, 1861

Centralisation of the means of production and socialisation of labour at last reach a point where they become incompatible with their capitalist membrane. . . . Capitalist production begets, with the inexorability of a law of nature, its own negation.
—KARL MARX, *Capital*, Vol. I, 32, 1867

Worthy work carries with it the hope of pleasure in rest, the hope of the pleasure in our using what it makes, and the hope of pleasure in our daily creative skill. All other work but this is worthless; it is slaves' work – mere toiling to live, that we may live to toil.
—WILLIAM MORRIS, "Useful Work versus Useless Toil," lecture delivered January 16, 1884

The moment a man gets money, so many men are trying to get it away from him that in a little while he regards the whole human race as his enemy, and he generally thinks that they could be rich too if they only attend to business as he has.
—ROBERT G. INGERSOLL, *A Lay Sermon*, 1886

The crying need of the nation is not for better morals, cheaper bread, temperance, liberty, culture, redemption of fallen sisters and erring brothers, nor the grace, love, and fellowship of the Trinity, but simply for enough money. And the evil to be attacked is not sin, suffering, greed, priestcraft, kingcraft, demagogy, monopoly, ignorance, drink, war, pestilence, nor any of the consequences of poverty, but just poverty itself.
—GEORGE BERNARD SHAW, *Major Barbara*, "Preface," 1907

Whoever consumes goods or services without producing by personal effort the equivalent of what he or she consumes, inflicts on the community precisely the same injury as a thief, and would, in any honest state, be treated as a thief, however full his or her pockets might be of money made by other people.
—GEORGE BERNARD SHAW, *Misalliance*, "Preface," 1914

I call machinery the greatest of emancipators. I will go farther and say that human slavery will not have been fully abolished until every task now accomplished by human hands is turned out by some machine, if it can be done as well or better by a machine.
—THOMAS A. EDISON, *The Diary and Sundry Observations* (1948), 1926

The rationality of the system of production, in its technical aspects, is accompanied by the irrationality of our system of production in its social aspects. Economic crises, unemployment, war, govern man's fate.
—ERICH FROMM, *Escape from Freedom*, 4, 1941

The first essential for economists . . . is to . . . combat, not foster, the ideology which pretends that values which can be measured in terms of money are the only ones that ought to count.
—JOAN ROBINSON, *Economic Philosophy*, "What Are the Rules of the Game?" 1962

Unlimited economic growth has the marvelous quality of stilling discontent while maintaining privilege.
—NOAM CHOMSKY, *For Reasons of State*, "Introduction," 1973

Growth for the sake of growth is the ideology of the cancer cell. Cancer has no purpose but growth; but it does have another result – the death of the host.
—EDWARD ABBEY, *One Life at a Time, Please*, "Arizona: How Big is Big Enough?" 1988

Marriage. Family

It [marriage] may be compared to a cage; the birds outside are desperately anxious to get in, and those that are in it are equally anxious to get out.
—MICHEL DE MONTAIGNE, *Essays* (Trechman transl.), III, 5, 1588

Where there's marriage without love, there will be love without marriage.
—BENJAMIN FRANKLIN, *Poor Richard's Almanack*, 1734

One good Husband is worth two good Wives; for the scarcer things are the more they're valued.

—BENJAMIN FRANKLIN, *Poor Richard's Almanack*, 1742

The liberty of divorces is not only a cure to hatred and domestic quarrels; it is also an admirable preservative against them, and the only secret for keeping alive that love which first united the married couple.

—DAVID HUME, *Essays Moral and Political*, "Of Polygamy and Divorces," 1742

The *divine right* of husbands, like the divine right of kings, may, it is hoped in this enlightened age, be contested without danger.

—MARY WOLLSTONECRAFT, *A Vindication of the Rights of Woman*, 3, 1792

The absurd duty, too often inculcated, of obeying a parent only on account of his being a parent, shackles the mind and prepares it for a slavish submission to any power but reason.

—MARY WOLLSTONECRAFT, *A Vindication of the Rights of Woman*, 11, 1792

With family governments as with political ones, a harsh despotism itself generates a great part of the crimes it has to repress; while on the other hand a mild and liberal rule both avoids many causes of dissension, and so ameliorates the tone of feeling as to diminish the tendency to transgression.

—HERBERT SPENCER, *Education*, 3, 1861

Human Affairs

Marriage must be a relation either of sympathy or of conquest.
—GEORGE ELIOT, *Romola*, 48, 1863

Man scans with scrupulous care the character and pedigree of his horses, cattle, and dogs before he matches them; but when he comes to his own marriage he rarely, or never, takes any such care.
—CHARLES DARWIN, *The Descent of Man*, 21, 1871

I believe in the fireside. I believe in the democracy of home. I believe in the republicanism of the family.
—ROBERT G. INGERSOLL, *Liberty of Man, Woman, and Child*, 1877

The first class antagonism which appears in history coincides with the development of the antagonism between man and woman in monogamian marriage, and the first class oppression with that of the female sex by the male.
—FRIEDRICH ENGELS, *The Origin of the Family, Private Property, and the State*, 1884

Civilization commences at the hearthstone. When intelligence rocks the cradle – when the house is filled with philosophy and kindness – you will see a world at peace.
—ROBERT G. INGERSOLL, Interview, *New York World*, 1888

The child learns more of the virtues needed in modern life – of fairness, of justice, of comradeship, of collective interest and action – in a common school than can be taught in the most perfect family circle.
—CHARLOTTE PERKINS GILMAN, *Women and Economics*, 13, 1898

All these reverend gentlemen who insist on the word "obey" in the marriage service should be removed for a clear violation of the Thirteenth Amendment to the Federal Constitution, which says there shall be neither slavery nor involuntary servitude within the United States.
—ELIZABETH CADY STANTON, *Eighty Years and More*, 1898

Science . . . must put it in the power of woman to decide for herself whether she will or will not become a mother. This is the solution of the whole question. This frees woman. The babes that are then born will be welcome.
—ROBERT G. INGERSOLL, *What Is Religion?* 8, 1899

All that is exchanged between husband and wife in their life together . . . can never be demanded by one or the other as a right.
—ELLEN KEY, *The Morality of Woman and Other Essays*, "The Morality of Woman," 1911

After some generations . . . we shall see marriages such as even now are seen, in which not observation of a duty but liberty itself is the pledge that assures fidelity.
—ELLEN KEY, *The Morality of Woman and Other Essays*, "The Morality of Woman," 1911

Physically there is nothing to distinguish human society from the farm-yard except that children are more troublesome and costly than chickens and women are not so completely enslaved as farm stock.
—GEORGE BERNARD SHAW, *Getting Married*, "Preface," 1911

Human Affairs

From the time of puberty onward the individual must devote himself to the great task of *freeing himself from the parents*; and only after this detachment is accomplished can he cease to be a child and become a member of the social community.

—SIGMUND FREUD, *A General Introduction to Psychoanalysis*, 21, 1917

Being the most sacred aspect of woman's freedom, voluntary motherhood is motherhood in its highest and holiest form.

—MARGARET SANGER, *Woman and the New Race*, 18, 1920

The difficulty about our family system remains: adults need quiet, order, and cleanliness; and children need noise, dirt, and destructiveness.

—GEORGE BERNARD SHAW, letter to E. Margaret Wheeler, March 1, 1945

Marriage should be a combining of two whole, independent existences, not a retreat, an annexation, a flight, a remedy.

—SIMONE DE BEAUVOIR, *The Second Sex*, 16, 1949

A large proportion of mankind, like pigeons and partridges, on reaching maturity, having passed through a period of playfulness and promiscuity, establish what they hope and expect will be a permanent and fertile mating relationship. This we call marriage.

—C. D. DARLINGTON, *Genetics and Man*, 1964

Consider the standard two-person married couple. . . . They will *share* a VCR, a microwave, etc. This is not a matter of ideology or even personal inclination. It is practically the definition of marriage. Marriage is socialism among two people.

—BARBARA EHRENREICH, *The Worst Years of our Lives* (1990), "Socialism in One Household," 1987

Women. Gender

Women, commonly called Ladies, . . . are not allowed to exert any manual strength, and from them the negative virtues only are expected: patience, docility, good humor, and flexibility; virtues incompatible with any vigorous exertion of intellect.

—MARY WOLLSTONECRAFT, *A Vindication of the Rights of Woman*, 1792

Would man but generously snap our chains, and be content with rational fellowship instead of slavish obedience, they would find us more observant daughters, more affectionate sisters, more faithful wives, more reasonable mothers – in a word, better citizens. We should love them with true affection, because we should learn to respect ourselves.

—MARY WOLLSTONECRAFT, *A Vindication of the Rights of Woman*, 9, 1792

I do not wish them to have power over men; but over themselves.

—MARY WOLLSTONECRAFT, *A Vindication of the Rights of Woman*, 4, 1792.

Male and female represent the two sides of the great radical dualism. But, in fact, they are perpetually passing into one another. Fluid hardens to solid, solid rushes to fluid. There is no wholly masculine man, no purely feminine woman.
—MARGARET FULLER, "The Great Lawsuit. . . ," *The Dial*, July, 1843

What woman needs is not as a woman to act or rule, but as a nature to grow, as an intellect to discern, as a soul to live freely and unimpeded, to unfold such powers as were given her when we left our common home.
—MARGARET FULLER, "The Great Lawsuit. . . ," *The Dial*, July, 1843

Resolved, That the same amount of virtue, delicacy, and refinement of behavior that is required of woman in the social state, should also be required of man, and the same transgressions should be visited with equal severity on both man and woman.
—WOMAN'S RIGHTS CONVENTION, "Declaration of Sentiments," Seneca Falls, N.Y., July 19-20, 1848. One of a number of resolutions passed

All political rights which it is expedient for man to exercise, it is equally so for women. . . . Our doctrine is that "right is of no sex."
—STEPHEN DOUGLASS, "The Rights of Women," *The North Star*, July 28, 1848

The masters of all other slaves rely, for maintaining obedience, on fear; either fear of themselves, or religious fears. The masters of

women wanted more than simple obedience, and they turned the whole force of education to effect their purpose.
—JOHN STUART MILL, *On the Subjection of Women*, 1, 1869

The idea of the women of America, (extricated from this daze, this fossil and unhealthy air which hangs about the word *lady*) develop'd, raised to become the robust equals, workers, and, it may be, even practical and political deciders with the men – greater than man, we may admit, through their divine maternity, always their towering, emblematic attribute – but great, at any rate, as man in all departments; or rather, capable of being so, soon as they realize it.
—WALT WHITMAN, *Democratic Vistas*, 1871

If the bird *does* like its cage, and *does* like its sugar and will not leave it, why keep the door so carefully shut? Why not open it, only a little? Do they know, there is many a bird will not break its wings against the bars, but would fly if the doors were open?
—OLIVE SCHREINER, *The Story of an African Farm*, II, 4, 1883

Woman is learning for herself that not self-sacrifice, but self-development, is her first duty in life; and this, not primarily for the sake of others but that she may become fully herself, a perfectly rounded being from every point of view.
—MATHILDA J. GAGE, *Woman, Church, and State*, 1893

The New Woman is a great improvement on the old. She loves the open air like a man, and is nearly as unconventional. There seems to be more poetry in her soul than in man's.
—JOHN BURROUGHS, *Journal*, May, 1897. Quoted in Barrus, *The Life and Letters of John Burroughs* (1925)

The labor of women in the house, certainly, enables men to produce more wealth than they otherwise could; and in this way women are economic factors in society. But so are horses.
—CHARLOTTE PERKINS GILMAN, *Women and Economics*, I, 1898

Merely external emancipation has made of the modern woman an artificial being. . . . Now, woman is confronted with the necessity of emancipating herself from emancipation, if she really desires to be free.
—EMMA GOLDMAN, *Anarchism and Other Essays*, "The Tragedy of Women's Emancipation," 1910

Our humanness is a quality common to both sexes, and the evil of the previous position of women is that they were confined to the exercise of sex faculties only – however nobly developed – and denied the exercise of the human ones.
—CHARLOTTE PERKINS GILMAN, "On Ellen Key and the Woman Movement," *The Forerunner,* February, 1913

Woman's role has been that of an incubator and little more. She has given birth to an incubated race.
—MARGARET SANGER, *Woman and the New Race*, 18, 1920

The future woman must have a life work and economic independence. She must have knowledge. She must have the right of motherhood at her own discretion. The present mincing horror at free womanhood must pass if we are ever to be rid of the bestiality of free manhood.
—W. E. B. DUBOIS, *Darkwater: Voices from Within the Veil*, "The Damnation of Women," 1920

Great Freethinkers

Women have served all these centuries as looking glasses possessing the magic and delicious power of reflecting the figure of man at twice its natural size.
—VIRGINIA WOOLF, *A Room of One's Own*, 2, 1929

One is not born, but rather becomes a woman. No biological, psychological, or economic fate determines the figure that the human female presents in society; it is civilization as a whole that produces this creature, intermediate between male and eunuch, which is described as feminine.
—SIMONE DE BEAUVOIR, *The Second Sex*, 12, 1949

It is not in giving life but in risking life that man is raised above the animal; that is why superiority has been accorded in humanity not to the sex that brings forth but to that which kills.
—SIMONE DE BEAUVOIR, *The Second Sex*, 4, 1949

Woman's homosexuality is one attempt among others to reconcile her autonomy with the passivity of her flesh.
—SIMONE DE BEAUVOIR, *The Second Sex*, 15, 1949

Noncommitment and vicarious living are . . . at the very heart of our conventional definition of femininity.
—BETTY FRIEDAN, *The Feminine Mystique*, 12, 1963

Patriarchy has a . . . powerful hold through its successful habit of passing itself off as nature.
—KATE MILLETT, *Sexual Politics*, 1969

Nothing short of equality will do *and* . . . in a society marred by injustice and cruelty, equality will never be good enough.
—BARBARA EHRENREICH, *The Worst Years of Our Lives* (1990), "Why We Lost the ERA," 1986

Race

The whole commerce between master and slave is a perpetual exercise of the most boisterous passions, the most unremitting despotism on the one part, and degrading submission on the other. . . . Indeed, I tremble for my country when I reflect that God is just; that his justice cannot sleep forever.
—THOMAS JEFFERSON, *Notes on the State of Virginia*, 18, 1787

I have observed this in my experience of slavery, that whenever my condition was improved, instead of its increasing my contentment, it only increased my desire to be free, and set me to thinking of plans to gain my freedom. I have found that, to make a contented slave, it is necessary to make a thoughtless one. It is necessary to darken his moral and mental vision, and, as far as possible, to annihilate the power of reason.
—FREDERICK DOUGLASS, *Narrative of the Life of Frederick Douglass, an American Slave*, 10, 1845

Slavery proved as injurious to her [my mistress slaveholder] as it did to me. When I went there, she was a pious, warm, and tenderhearted woman. . . . Slavery soon proved its ability to divest her of

these heavenly qualities. Under its influence, the tender heart became stone, and the lamblike disposition gave way to one of tiger-like fierceness.
—FREDERICK DOUGLASS, *Narrative of the Life of Frederick Douglass, an American Slave*, 7, 1845

I will hear nothing of degradation or of ignorance against the black man. If he knows enough to be hanged, he knows enough to vote.
—FREDERICK DOUGLASS, "Our Work Is Not Done," speech to the American Anti-Slavery Society, Philadelphia, December 3-4, 1863

It is a peculiar sensation, this double-consciousness, this sense of always looking at one's self through the eyes of others, of measuring one's soul by the tape of a world that looks on in amused contempt and pity. One ever feels his two-ness: an American, a Negro; two souls, two thoughts, two unreconciled strivings; two warring ideals in one dark body, whose dogged strength alone keeps it from being torn asunder.
—W. E. B. DUBOIS, *The Souls of Black Folks*, 1, 1903

To be a poor man is hard, but to be a poor race in a land of dollars is the very bottom of hardships.
—W. E. B. DUBOIS, *The Souls of Black Folks*, 1, 1903

For generations in the mind of America, the Negro has been more of a formula than a human being – a something to be argued about, condemned or defended, to be "kept down," or "in his place," or "helped up," to be worried with or worried over, harrassed or patronized, a social bogey or a social burden.
—ALAIN LOCKE, *The New Negro*, 1925

It is the duty of the younger Negro artist . . . to change through the forces of his art that old whispering "I want to be white," hidden in the aspirations of his people, to "Why should I want to be white? I am a Negro – and beautiful!"
—LANGSTON HUGHES, "The Negro Artist and the Racial Mountain," *The Nation*, June 23, 1926

We have within us as a race new stirrings; stirrings of the beginning of a new appreciation of joy, of a new desire to create, of a new will to be; as though in this morning of group life we had awakened from some sleep that at once dimly mourns the past and dreams a splendid future.
—W. E. B. DUBOIS, "Criteria of Negro Art," *The Crisis*, October, 1926

I did not feel the rhythms of the primitive surging through me, and so I could not live and write as though I did. I was only an American Negro – who had loved the surface of Africa and the rhythms of Africa – but I was not Africa. I was Chicago and Kansas City and Broadway and Harlem.
—LANGSTON HUGHES, *The Big Sea*, "Not Primitive," 1940

The process of averaging the characters of a given group, knocking the individuals together, giving them a good stirring, and then serving the resulting omelet as a "race" is essentially the anthropological process of race-making. . . . It is an omelet which corresponds to nothing in nature.
—ASHLEY MONTAGU, "The Meaninglessness of the Anthropological Conception of Race," *Journal of Heredity*, 23, 1941

I have been in Sorrow's kitchen and licked out all the pots. . . . What I had to swallow in the kitchen has not made me less glad to have lived, nor made me want to low-rate the human race, nor any whole sections of it. I take no refuge from myself in bitterness.
—ZORA NEALE HURSTON, *Dust Tracks on a Road*, 16, 1942

Negro blood is sure powerful – because just *one* drop of black blood makes a colored man. *One* drop – you are a Negro! . . . Black is powerful.
—LANGSTON HUGHES, *Simple Takes a Wife*, 1953

This is something that I challenge very deeply, and very sincerely, the fact that the success of a few Negroes, including myself or Jackie Robinson, can make up . . . for $700 a year for thousands of Negro families in the South. My father was a slave, and I have cousins who are sharecroppers, and I do not see my success in terms of myself.
—PAUL ROBESON, testimony before the House Un-American Activities Committee, July 13, 1956

"Gradualism" is a mighty long road. It stretches back 100 long and weary years, and looking forward it has no end. . . . The viewpoint that progress must be slow is rooted in the idea that democratic rights, as far as Negroes are concerned, are not inalienable and self-evident as they are for white Americans.
—PAUL ROBESON, *Here I Stand*, 4, 1958

It comes as a great shock around the age of 5, 6, or 7. . . . to see Gary Cooper killing off the Indians and, although you are rooting for Gary Cooper, that the Indians are you.
—JAMES BALDWIN, speech at Cambridge University, February 17, 1965, *The New York Times Magazine*, March 7, 1965

What the Black Man must do now is look down at the ground upon which he stands, and claim it as his own. It is not abstract. Look down! Pick up the earth, or jab your fingernails into the concrete. It is real and it is yours, if you want it.
—AMIRI BARAKA, *Home: Social Essays*, "The Legacy of Malcolm X, and the Coming of the Black Nation," 1966

We must learn to lift as we climb.
—ANGELA DAVIS, *Women, Culture, and Politics*, 1989

Class

The difference of natural talents in different men is, in reality, much less than we are aware of; and the very different genius which appears to distinguish men of different profession . . . is not upon many occasions so much the cause as the effect of the division of labour. The difference . . . between a philosopher and a common street porter, for example, seems to arise not so much from nature as from habit, custom, and education.
—ADAM SMITH, *The Wealth of Nations*, I, 2, 1776

The preposterous distinctions of rank, which render civilization a curse by dividing the world between voluptuous tyrants and cunning devious dependents, corrupt almost equally every class of people.
—MARY WOLLSTONECRAFT, *A Vindication of the Rights of Woman*, 10, 1792

Freeman and slave, patrician and plebeian, lord and serf, guild-master and journeyman, in a word, oppressor and oppressed, stood in constant opposition to one another, carried on an uninterrupted, now hidden, now open fight, a fight that each time ended either in a revolutionary reconstitution of society at large, or in the common ruin of the contending classes.

—KARL MARX & FRIEDRICH ENGELS, *Manifesto of the Communist Party*, 1, 1848

Masses are rude, lame, unmade, pernicious in their demands and influence, and need not to be flattered but to be schooled. I wish not to concede anything to them, but to tame, drill, divide, and break them up, and draw individuals out of them.

—RALPH WALDO EMERSON, *The Conduct of Life*, "Considerations by the Way," 1860

He who before was the money-owner now strides in front as capitalist; the possessor of labour-power follows as his labourer. The one with an air of importance, smirking, intent on business; the other, timid and holding back, like one who is bringing his own hide to market and has nothing to expect but – a hiding.

—KARL MARX, *Capital*, Vol. I, 2, 6, 1867

There are wise people who talk ever so knowingly and complacently about "the working classes," and satisfy themselves that a day's hard intellectual work is very much harder than a day's hard manual toil, and are righteously entitled to much bigger pay. . . . But I know all about both; and so far as I am concerned, there isn't money enough in the universe to hire me to swing a pickax thirty days.

—MARK TWAIN, A *Connecticut Yankee in King Arthur's Court*, 28, 1889

A poor man who is ungrateful, unthrifty, discontented, and rebellious, is probably a real personality, and has much in him. . . . As for the virtuous poor, one can pity them of course, but one cannot possibly admire them. They have made private terms with the enemy, and sold their birthright for very bad pottage.
—OSCAR WILDE, "The Soul of Man under Socialism," *Fortnightly Review*, February, 1891

There is only one class in the community that thinks more about money than the rich, and that is the poor. The poor can think of nothing else. That is the misery of being poor.
—OSCAR WILDE, "The Soul of Man under Socialism," *Fortnightly Review*, February, 1891

In order to hold the esteem of men it is not sufficient merely to possess wealth or power. The wealth or power must be put in evidence, for esteem is awarded only on evidence.
—THORSTEIN VEBLEN, *The Theory of the Leisure Class*, 1899

Don't forget that, whilst you may nationalize the railroads in one afternoon, it will take a long time to transform all the third-class carriages and all the first-class carriages into second-class carriages.
—GEORGE BERNARD SHAW, words remembered by Sidney Webb, late 19th century. Quoted in Henderson, *George Bernard Shaw, Man of the Century* (1956)

Distance, n. The only thing that the rich are willing for the poor to call theirs, and keep.
—AMBROSE BIERCE, *The Devil's Dictionary*, 1906

The difference between a lady and a flower girl is not how she behaves, but how she's treated.
—GEORGE BERNARD SHAW, Eliza Doolittle in *Pygmalion*, V, 1916

I am willing to be charged with almost anything, rather than to be charged with being a leader. . . . I would be ashamed to admit that I had risen from the ranks. When I rise it will be with the ranks, not from the ranks.
—EUGENE V. DEBS, speech delivered on June 16, 1918

I asked a man in prison once how he happened to be there and he said he had stolen a pair of shoes. I told him if he had stolen a railroad he would be a United States Senator.
—MOTHER JONES, quoted in Parton, *The Autobiography of Mother Jones*, 1925

It is only because miners sweat their guts out that superior persons can remain superior.
—GEORGE ORWELL, *The Road to Wigan Pier*, 2, 1937

The defeats and victories of the fellows at the top aren't always defeats and victories for the fellows at the bottom.
—BERTOLT BRECHT, *Mother Courage*, III, 1939

This privation of parental love suffered during the tender years of childhood is probably one of the causes of the apparent "coldness," the seemingly unemotional character of the upper-class Englishman.
—ASHLEY MONTAGU, *On Being Human*, "What is the Nature of Human Nature?" 1950

One might summarize the newness of contemporary poverty by saying: These are the people who are immune to progress. . . . They are upside-down in the economy, and for them greater productivity often means worse jobs.
—MICHAEL HARRINGTON, *The Other America*, 1, 1962

A class of extemely rich people; another class of quite prosperous people (but nervous about the security of their situation); another class . . . living in desperation and misery within sight of colossal wealth. Who could be surprised that crime, violence, and drug addiction would accompany such contrasts?
—HOWARD ZINN, *Declarations of Independence: Cross-Examining American Ideology*, 7, 1990

Biographical Index

This index includes brief biographical information on all contributors. Numbers refer to page numbers of entries. Terms describing an author's philosophical stance provide a rough evaluation based on the best available sources.